Kelsey
FROM PAIN TO TRIUMPH

By: Phyllis Clemmons

McClure Publishing, Inc.
Bloomingdale, Illinois

Copyright © 2013

All rights reserved. Printed and bound in the United States of America. According to the 1976 United States Copyright Act, no part of this book may be reproduced or utilized in any form or by any means, electronic or mechanical, including photocopying, recording, or by any information storage or retrieval system, except by a reviewer who may quote brief passages in a review to be printed in a magazine or newspaper, without permission in writing from the Publisher: Inquiries should be addressed to McClure Publishing, Inc. Permissions Department, 358 West Army Trail Road, #205, Bloomingdale, Illinois 60108. Publication date: September 15, 2013.

Scripture quotations are taken from the Holy Bible, New Living Translation, copyright ©1996, 2004, 2007 by Tyndale House Foundation. Used by permission of Tyndale House Publishers, Inc., Carol Stream, Illinois 60188. All rights reserved.

The author and publisher have made every effort to ensure the accuracy and completeness of information contained in this book, we assume no responsibility for errors, inaccuracies, omissions, or any inconsistency therein.

ISBN 13: 978-0-9833697-9-0

LCCN: 2013950588

Cover Design Image by Jaime Duplass (123rf.com)
Interior Layout by Kathy McClure

http://www.mcclurepublishing.com

To order additional copies, please contact
mcclurepublishing@msn.com
800-659-4908

DEDICATION

I would like to dedicate this book to my three children: Darlene, Michelle and Brandi as a legacy of the power of prayer and faith that will serve them throughout the history of our family. A legacy that will encourage and strengthen them as well as, my grandchildren, my great grandchildren and all the children of this family for generations to come. May the blessings and favor of God be upon you all.

ACKNOWLEDGMENT

To my Lord and Savior, Jesus Christ, I give you glory, honor and praise. I thank you Lord for giving me the courage to become transparent, baring my very soul so that others might be inspired, encouraged and hopeful by what I have shared from some of the darkest days of my life, so that this project will serve them in the darkest days of their lives.

To my loving husband, Melvin and my wonderful granddaughter, Asiah thank you both for allowing me to take precious family time away from you to complete this project.

To all the pastors, leaders and mentors that (by way of the word of God and as a godly example), have seeded and watered into the fertile ground of my inner woman. Bless each and every one of you for being instrumental in the harvest of who I have become today as well as what I am yet becoming.

To the Sisters In the Spirit who are my prayer partners and have been instrumental in keeping me grounded throughout the past 20 years, thank you all for always being there.

To my BFF and confidant, Brenda for always giving me Godly counsel, (even when it was painful). Thank you for always keeping it real.

TABLE OF CONTENT

I.   Tender Roots
   1. In the Beginning
   2. Daddy's Provision
   3. Rusty
   4. New Found Friends

II.   Early Childhood Antics
   5. False Alarm
   6. Liar, Liar Pants on Fire
   7. Dippin Snuff

III. The Burden of Childhood Baggage
   8. Trouble in the Camp
   9. Emotional Trauma
   10. Late Foundational Training
   11. Midnight Madness
   12. No Rhyme or Reason
   13. Basement "Time Out"
   14. Motherless Child
   15. Out of Control

IV.   God Steps in Right on Time
   16. Defiance at its Peak
   17. The Last Straw
   18. A time of Transition
   19. Holding Pattern
   20. Falcon Boarding School for Girls
   21. Acclimation Process

      22. Two Year Turn Around
      23. The Next Level of Transition
      24. Meet and Greet

V.   **Favor, Grace and Mercy in His Sight**
      25. Another Chance
      26. A New Family
      27. Settling into the Routine
      28. Dr. Jekyll
      29. Marriage Proposal
      30. Darby Bound
      31. Mr. Hyde

CONCLUSION

Foreword

Beloved, it is my heartfelt desire that my story will bring inspiration, encouragement and hope, that no matter what challenges, trials and tribulations you face throughout your lifetime, that all who read the pages within this book will have the assurance of knowing without a shadow of a doubt that God has promised to deliver you out of every situation. He was and still is today faithful to deliver me out of mine, and He will do the same for you. His word tells us that he is no respecter of persons.

Know that life is greater than your circumstances and more than your sufferings. I pray that my story will lift you up and support you through your darkest hour and that it will bring you to a place of knowing that there is a way to go through the fire and not even smell the smoke when you have reached the other side.

Know that with God as your help you can experience greater strength, greater hope and greater trust that will help you to overcome and triumph over all the hard times that you will ever face.

Give your life to Him, knowing that when unexpected circumstances knock at your door, you can answer the door with confidence because of who we are and whose we are. Your Father in heaven is always there and never leaves you without access to his love, wisdom, guidance and comfort. His word says that you have all that you need for life and for godliness.

It is my hope that not only in your times of pain but also in your times of triumph, you will come to him in prayer with a trusting, thankful and open heart and mind that is receptive to the presence of His Spirit, guiding and directing your path.

II Corinthians 4:17-18 (NLT)

"For our present troubles are small and won't last very long. Yet they produce for us a glory that vastly outweighs them and will last forever! So we don't look at the troubles we can see now; rather, we fix our gaze on things that cannot be seen. For the things we see now will soon be gone, but the things we cannot see will last forever."

It is critical in life to always have the presence of mind to know that hard times come and go, (giving emphasis on hard times going). Learning that through the grace of God, we don't have to hold on with teeth tightly gritted together and white knuckles while we are going through various trials and tribulations; but we can have a sense of peace and the ability to flourish during those times by channeling our focus toward Jesus, "... the author and finisher of our faith;..." (Hebrews 12:2).

The Bible calls them temporary, light afflictions. This lets us know that it's only for a season and that it is not beyond what we are able to bear. For our Creator is thoroughly acquainted with our frame, our mind, our will and our emotions, to the point that He is able to accurately assess just how much we can handle without going one tittle over what we are built to endure.

These afflictions, though painful at the time do have value. For me, the value lies in future trials being supported by a structurally sound faith from historically victorious outcomes of former trials that occurred along life's journey.

God is frugal, in that He uses all of our life's experiences (good and bad). Even when it doesn't feel good, it will ultimately work for our good and is useful for molding and shaping us into what we will ultimately become. Our upward development brings honor to God and favor with people in that they might see our faith and works together and be persuaded toward salvation.

This book is an autobiography of my life from when I was a small child until 17 years old. It reveals some tragedies and triumphs of how I got through some of the most painful times of my life.

Tender Roots

Chapter 1

In the Beginning

Standing outside the hospital looking toward the revolving doorway before going in, I begin to think about my baby brother who had just arrived. As my Dad and I approached the maternity ward after getting off the elevator, we were told that only children 12 years and older were permitted in the maternity ward. Thoughts about how my only sibling looked and how it was going to affect me, raced through my mind. Even at the tender age of four, I had a perception about life that was very insightful. The addition to the family would change everything; I knew things were not going to remain the same.

Dad borrowed his friend's car the day Mom and the baby were due to come home from the hospital. He did not want to bring Mom and my new baby brother home in a taxi and we didn't have a car of our own at the time. Dad and I were both anxious as we drove to pick them up. Afterward, we returned home and Dad pulled up to the curb to park the car. He got out and walked around the front of the car and opened the car door to help Mom and my baby brother out. He then helped me out of the car and we proceeded to enter the 5 story tenement building on King Street in Philadelphia, PA. We lived in the rear apartment, so it took us a little time to walk to the back of the building. The living room doubled as my bedroom and my bed was a pull out sofa. My parent's bedroom was adjacent to the living room and a crib for my baby brother was set up in their room on the wall by the door. Due to the close proximity of those two rooms, I was exposed to many types of adult sounds and conversations at a very early age that were not meant for my ear gates and would prove to be instrumental in developing some very unhealthy thought processes in future years to come.

An elderly woman lived in the first floor front apartment. She was an asset to some of the good qualities I developed over the years. Mrs. India was a widow whose husband died before I got to really know her. As I passed her apartment to get to the rear, Mrs. India always exemplified kindheartedness toward me.

In the fall of the following year, I began kindergarten. I was very excited about this new venture. It gave me a small bit of independence and encouraged me to plead with my Mother to allow me to walk to school by myself.

After several months of her accompanying me, she finally relented under the conditions that I would walk the three blocks to school and would make no detours along the way. I agreed and the following Monday, I began my journey. As I walked, I would periodically look behind me and catch little glimpses of her darting behind trees as she followed me from a distance until I was safely inside the school building. This became our daily routine until Mom was confident that I could go and come home from school successfully, without supervision.

Now winter was very cold and in spite of the wool gloves I wore, my fingers ached from the cold and by the time I ran the three long blocks home, I was in tears.

Kelsey from Pain to Triumph

Mrs. India saw me from her window where she sat every afternoon and began to knock on the window and beckon me to come into the building. By the time I ran up the front steps into the building, she would be at her apartment door. "Come in here Chile and let me warm yo hands," she would say, often leaving off the last part of most of her words like "chile" instead of child and "yo" instead of "your." Mrs. India would take my gloves off and put my little hands between hers as she gently began to rub them back and forth, intermittently putting her hands on the hot radiator for maximum heat and once again rubbing my hands between hers until my hands were warm and the stiffness was gone. The only thing that remained from the incident was my tear stained face and a snotty nose.

Mrs. India would give me toilet tissue to wipe my nose and then proceed to pleasure my palate with homemade cookies and milk. I ate and drank with sheer abandonment. "Gon home to yo' Momma now," she would say and I would bid her goodbye and scurry off to the rear apartment.

I recall once (after I was thoroughly familiar with the route to and from school) I had decided I wasn't going to go straight home but I would go to a classmate's house after school for cookies and milk and a short play time. I got so engrossed in playing that I totally lost track of time. Several hours had passed when I was reminded by my classmate's mother, "Kelsey, does your mother know where you are?" I said, "No Ma'am." She then told me that she thought I should be going home as she was sure my Mother would be worried by now. I was only 5 years old at the time.

Reality suddenly struck me that she must be right in her assessment, and I bid them goodbye and went skipping off toward home. As I was coming down our street, I saw Mom standing in the doorway with a frantic look on her face. As our eyes met, her expression changed to one I had not seen before. It was not a pleasant face and she said, "Get in here young lady, where have you been? I have been worried sick and looking for you for the past two hours." Mom grabbed me by the ear and marched me swiftly to the rear apartment. While on my tip toes I attempted to explain that I stopped at a friend's home for what started out to be a brief visit but I lost track of time. Mom had never spanked me before, but she never wanted me to do that again. I figured what I had done was a serious no no. I received by way of a spanking, a very strong and compelling suggestion not to stop between school and home without permission again.

My first and only spanking from my Daddy was due to a beautiful bedspread he bought for my Mother. One night when they wanted to watch TV in the living room where I normally slept, I was allowed to sleep in my parent's bed. While in bed, I noticed the new spread had one fringe at the beginning hanging lower than the others. I thought that I would pull it off so that all remaining fringes would be even.

As I pulled the first one, the fringes began to unravel one at a time until that whole side of the spread's fringes was completely unraveled. Needless to say, 'it was smoke in the city' that night as my Daddy applied hand to backside after he saw the mess I had made of the new bedspread. I don't ever remember my Daddy being so angry.

Chapter 2

Daddy's Provision

My Daddy brought Mom a washing machine which was the state of the art machine during that time. It had two rollers at the top called a wringer and was used to feed pieces of freshly washed, wet clothing from the machine after going through the agitation process. The wringer would squeeze much of the water out by the time the article of clothing would reach the back side of the machine.

According to today's standards this appeared to me to be a slow arduous process, but Mom was happy to be able to do the laundry without having to scrub clothes on a wash board which was the norm for most households of that era.

As I look back, I believe it to be an accurate assumption that my Father, a young taxi cab driver who had spent time in the Korean War; worked hard to give my Mother the best that he was able to afford. I have come to this conclusion as I knew from visiting the other neighborhood kids' apartments that we were first in our neighborhood to have a black and white TV as well as the brand new washing machine and a stove with a pancake grill made right in the center of it. Life was great.

Chapter 3

Rusty

Once Mom realized that Mrs. India had taken a strong liking to me, she began to solicit her for babysitting duty, mostly on weekends. She hardly ever had to worry about a sitter for my baby brother Tony as my Daddy's sister, Aunt Lee and her husband, Uncle J.T. would come almost every weekend and take my brother Tony to their house for the weekend. She was crazy about that little scrawny high yellow boy. So much so, that she eventually stopped bringing him back home. My parents didn't seem to mind much. I guess they had their hands full with me and were grateful for the break.

I felt like an only child again, Daddy even bought me a puppy. I named him Rusty and he became my best friend and companion. We played together constantly. Rusty's dog treats were kept in the kitchen in the bottom of Mom's china cabinet. The top of the cabinet had double glass doors and Mom kept her good dishes and glassware displayed in that part of the cabinet. The bottom part had wooden doors that were great for swinging on. I never missed an opportunity to swing on those two bottom doors whenever I got Rusty his dog treats.

One day, while I was swinging on the cabinet doors, the whole cabinet began to tip over and before I knew it the cabinet had fallen on top of me. Fortunately, I was not hurt.

I started to cry because all of Mom's good china came crashing to the floor. Glass and china chards went everywhere. I just knew Mom was going to beat me senseless. To my surprise when she ran into the kitchen; the look I saw on her face was one of fear not anger.

She bent over and began to lift the cabinet up enough to pull me from under it. She then picked me up and held me close to her breast. I can still remember how hard and fast her heart was beating. She looked at me and said, "Kelsey, are you okay?"

She started to inspect my body from head to toe for cuts and bruises. We were both surprised that I had none. Mom laid me down on her bed. She usually put me down for a nap whenever she needed a break from me and my shenanigans, (I think sometimes it was a bit overwhelming for her).

I could hear her in the kitchen as she began the tedious process of cleaning up the mess I caused. I was grateful for the nap that day. It was a much better fate then the beating I had visualized as Mom had told me over and over again not to swing on the cabinet doors. That day I was relieved to be placed in the safe harbor of Mom's bed and shortly afterward, I was fast asleep.

The strong companionship Rusty and I shared would soon come to an abrupt end. One day, Rusty ran away after the backyard gate was carelessly left opened. Daddy looked for him for many days after, but he was not successful in finding him. For a while, I cried myself to sleep at night but as the days turned into weeks and the weeks turned into months, I began to accept the fact that Rusty was not coming back. One day months later, Daddy came home all excited with a big dog. Daddy had the biggest grin on his face. He said, "Kelsey, look who I found, it's Rusty."

The animal that stood before me with his tongue hanging out of his mouth panting with a wild look in his eyes and much bigger than I remembered him, was unrecognizable.

He was twice the size of the Rusty I remembered and appeared to be very aggressive. His coat was dirty and a bit patchy as if he had been in a scrape or two over the previous months.

I totally did not take to the "new" Rusty and stood behind Mom holding on to her skirt tail. I told my Daddy "that's not Rusty." Daddy was not able to convince me otherwise and so he reluctantly took Rusty away and I never saw him again. I didn't ask where he had taken him, but I did feel a sense of relief that he was gone.

Chapter 4

New Found Friends

After Rusty was gone, I turned my attention toward the human aspects of companionship. By then I was six years old. There were more boys in our neighborhood than girls and frankly I seemed to share more commonalities with the boys. We would play with pogo sticks; climb over fences, up trees and shoot marbles.

All was well until the day that we all climbed the church gate. I was the last one to attempt to jump the gate but my shoe got caught as I tried to jump to the other side. One foot went down and the other foot didn't. The boys heard me scream and when they turned to see what happened, there I was hanging by one foot. They ran to my aide to help get my foot from between the gate spokes. My ankle hurt and I was not able to walk without support. They helped to support my weight as I put an arm around each ones shoulder and limped home. My ankle was sprained and I had to stay in the house for almost a week recovering from that incident.

Mom was not too happy about it and forbid me to play with the boys after that. That's when I started playing with Evie, Suzanne, Terry, Ella and Lisa. During that time there was a Baptist church down the street that began to recruit the neighborhood kids to come to Sunday school. We all began going every Sunday. They also had a children's ministry at the church. All the girls wanted to be on their children's usher board, but we were instructed that in order to be on the usher board we would need to give our lives to Christ and be baptized.

We all gave our life to Christ that same day. One of the church elders led us in the sinners prayer and afterward we were given a date for baptismal. The day we were scheduled to be baptized, all of us were given white robes and shower caps. As each of us went up to the baptismal pool, one of the church mothers whispered something in each girl's ear just before she stepped down into the water. When it was my turn, the church mother bent down and whispered in my ear to hold my breath before going down into the water. I was so young (six) at the time, that I remembered thinking to myself, "What does she mean?" (I didn't know what it meant to hold your breath). I stepped into the baptismal pool and the Pastor said, "I baptize you in the name of the Father, the Son and the Holy Ghost." He then reclined my body into the water. I quickly found out what it meant to hold your breath as I came up from the water sputtering, coughing and gasping for air.

We were now full-fledged members of Sharon Baptist Church. Now we could be on the children's usher board. We all had to wear white blouses and navy blue pleated skirts. The children's usher board was scheduled to usher once each month on the 4th Sunday. We were all pretty diligent with going to church each Sunday and ushering on the 4th Sunday for about 6 months. Sadly, Little by little we all started to fall away until eventually, we all stopped going completely.

It was at that point that I stopped playing with Evie, Suzanne, Terry and Ella. They were all a little younger than I was, and I no longer had an interest in playing their favorite games, (which were Hopscotch and Simon Says).

Lisa and I continued to be close and we did everything together. She was more like a cousin than a friend. Actually, Lisa's baby brother was one of my Uncle's children out of wedlock.

My Mom and Lisa's mom, (who I affectionately called Aunt Renee), were best friends. Aunt Renee lived in the apartment building right next door to us. Each morning before school, I would go by their house and eat shredded wheat cereal with them and wait for Lisa to get ready so we could walk to school together. Lisa also had an older brother, Butchie. He was mean as a snake and would take advantage of every opportunity to punch you hard in the arm displaying his handy work by leaving the evidence of a charley horse, (A cramp or stiffness of various muscles in the body that can be caused by injury).

Butchie had a raggedy dirty stuffed dog that he kept under his pillow at night. He had forbidden anyone to touch the dog. This seemed to be a challenge that I had trouble resisting, although I was well aware of the painful consequences of doing so. On more than one occasion, my arm was fair game for his wrath and though I was much younger than him, he showed me no mercy. As fate would have it, I lost track of that family due to circumstances beyond my control.

Over 50 years later, computer technology resulted in our crossing paths again. To my dismay, I discovered while in conversation with his wife, Butchie still had the stuffed dog; although the dog was no longer kept under his pillow. I laughed, thinking to myself how we sometimes have trouble letting things go that we should have left behind as we grow to new levels of maturity in our lives.

Lisa also spent too many years past it's time, still sucking her thumb. Let's just say, well after her toddler years, to put it mildly. As kids, we would spend hours playing dress up and doing and redoing our hair. Lisa was a master with the hot straightening comb and she kept my hair very nicely pressed, oiled with the hairdressing of that day, (Vaseline Petroleum Jelly), and my bangs curled.

One day Daddy came home from work with a gift for Lisa and me. It was two identical three piece gift sets that consisted of comb, brush and mirror, one set was yellow and the other pink.

Lisa was extra excited that day about playing beautician with the new comb, brush and mirror gift sets my Daddy bought us. I was the recipient of her hot curling iron skills. That day, while Lisa was curling my bangs; the hot curler handle slipped and I felt the searing hot burn made by the curling iron as it prominently displayed a burn mark across my forehead. Needless to say, I screamed and was so angry about the pain of the burn and the mark it left that I picked up her new mirror and threw it down on the floor.

The mirror shattered and broke into multiple pieces. That day we had our biggest fight ever. Harsh words were spoken between us, namely the "B" word escaped her lips as she saw her beautiful new mirror shattered on the floor. We did not play together for several days after that incident occurred. Lisa told my Daddy about what happened and he told me to apologize and give her my mirror since I broke hers. I was heartbroken about the mirror but I did what Daddy wanted and my friendship with Lisa was restored. We would continue our friendship until divine intervention would separate us and take us along different paths in life. I found Butchie first on a website that was instrumental in locating people with just a small bit of information as a lead.

Butchie then gave Lisa my telephone number and she called me shortly thereafter. Tears were shed during our telephone conversation as we walked down memory lane. I was sure that our relationship was about to be renewed. We talked a long time and then said our goodbyes. Lisa had just moved and her phone had not yet been connected. (She was calling me from someone else's phone but promised to call as soon as she got her new phone number). Years would go by again without a word from Lisa. I was alright with it though as I had a very strong sense in my spirit and knew that in life some relationships are only for a season. The season for my relationship with Lisa was apparently over for good and at that point I knew in my gut without a shadow of a doubt that I was not to try to rekindle it.

Isaiah 61:2-3 (NLT)

"To all who mourn in Israel, He will give a crown of beauty for ashes, a joyous blessing instead of mourning, festive praise instead of despair. In their righteousness, they will be like great oaks that the Lord has planted for his own glory."

The greatest revelation for those that start poorly, is in knowing that when all is said and done, we hold the power through Christ Jesus of choice and free will. We have the option of not staying in the same position that we started in. God's ordainment for our lives brings about a compulsion within us that causes those who are in him not to stay where we began but to strive to reach higher heights and deeper depths.

The question asked by some is, of all the trees God could have chosen to represent Israel in Isaiah 61:3, why did He choose the oak? I recall reading in one of my daily devotionals that those original oaks disappeared around AD 330. However, today there is an oak referred to as Abraham's Oak near Hebron. It is 23 feet (7 meters) around, and its foliage reaches a diameter of around 90 feet (27 meters). A few however, have reached a girth of 70 to 90 feet (21 to 27 meters). It is also said that King Arthur's Round Table was cut from a single slice of an oak tree. The slow-growing tree produces a hard, tough wood that is almost indestructible.

To me, that oak is symbolic of a seed planted when we make a choice to follow Christ. The more we grow in him through the instruction of his word, the more our spiritual tree produces and develops deeper roots and stronger, wider branches just like the oak of Hebron.

Early Childhood Antics

Chapter 5

False Alarm

In all fairness, before I can get into the most painful aspects of my childhood, I think it only prudent to give my audience some background of what I was like in those early days and how the lack of a good structural foundation played a role in how I behaved later in my preteen years, (age seven ½ - 12) when I was sent to live with Aunt Lee and Uncle J.T. As I look back on the time period from birth to age seven, I was under the care and leadership of my then young parents who I am sorry to say did not spend very much time through example or through instruction; teaching me those things that are necessary and instrumental in shaping one in good character traits. Nevertheless, I had no doubt that I was loved by my parents. This assumption was largely based on the affection displayed by both parents towards me. I suppose they did those things that they knew to do in reference to my care and upbringing.

The problem with that method of operation is as young parents that lacked a proper upbringing themselves, there were many aspects of child rearing that were not addressed because they had no prior reference points to guide them either by example or literary instruction known to them at the time. Therefore, I feel relatively comfortable in saying that through trial and error they did the best they could by me with the level of information known to them as young parents in their 20's.

One hot summer day while playing in the apartment building hallway next door to me, with all the neighborhood girls and boys; we spotted the fire alarm which in those days consisted of a small red case with a glass cover. It had a little hammer like instrument connected by a chain and attached to a hook on the hallway wall.

This contraption was displayed in the hallway on every floor of every apartment building. I remember one of the kids saying out loud, "I wonder if we hit that glass cover with that little hammer if the fire department would really come?" Of course we were curious and wanted to put it to the test. The only dilemma remaining was which one of us would be brave enough to remove the little hammer from the hook and break the glass? It seems that I could not resist an opportunity to put the fire alarm to the test and so I removed the hammer from the hook and hit the glass cover. It immediately shattered and a loud piercing, nonstop alarm filled the air.

We all stood there with our eyes wide with fear and the others began to look and point to me saying, "oooooh, look what you did." The neighbors began to look out of their apartment doors and many began their descent from the upper floors as it was the custom to do believing that some apartment in the building was on fire. Everyone was yelling above the alarm noise to attempt to glean some insight as to the nature of the fire. The kids all pointed to me and said, "Kelsey did it." I felt betrayed as if I had volunteered to assist them in this experimental venture and they all gave me up to save their own hides. In fear, I denied the allegation as I heard the fire truck sirens coming closer to the building. I began to sense that this was a serious crime I had committed and was at that point imagining that the police that followed the fire truck to the building had surely come to handcuff me and throw me in jail.

Someone went to the next building where I lived and got my Mother. The firemen talked to her and the neighbors. The children relayed the story to her of my crime. Of course, my Mother took me home and (you guessed it), put me down for a nap. I was relieved to sink down under the covers that engulfed me and provided a feeling of calmness and protection.

Mom kept me in the house for a while after that incident until the neighbors settled down and things were back to normal again.

Chapter 6

Liar, Liar Pants on Fire

From time to time I would spend weekends with one of my Grandmothers. My Daddy's Mom, (Grandma Chris) was not an educated woman and could not read or write. She had 11 children, (seven girls and four boys), my Daddy being the oldest son. In spite of her lack of education, she went to church regularly and had a good sense of application of the word of God and a strong commitment to prayer.

During the summer months, the tent meeting came to town. (Tent meeting was comprised of different Christian organizations that caravanned from town to town during the summer. They would set up a large tent on a vacant lot that they would rent for several days, preaching the word, handing out tracks, singing praise and worship songs and selling something called "liniment" at the end of each service). Many of the old folks back then went to tent meetings just for the liniment. It was thought to have some healing qualities and was used for arthritis, rheumatism, back and muscle aches and the like. Most would spend their last dollar for a bottle of the thick yellow oil.

Grandma Chris would drag us kids to tent meetings. It was always close enough to walk there and back and we did enjoy the singing. The preaching was mostly words of hell, fire and brimstone and we would giggle and make fun of the preacher whenever Grandma got so carried away by the word that she failed to pay much attention to what we were doing.

My visits to Grandma's meant I would be sleeping with her. I can close my eyes and still remember the medicinal smell of that liniment as she would rub it on her body each night fully expecting some relief from her aches and pains.

I can recall putting on my pajamas and jumping in the bed, ready to settle down for the night. Suddenly, the covers would be snatched from my body and Grandma would say, "Kelsey if you don't get out of that bed and get on your knees and say your prayers, you better," Whenever you came to her house you were expected to conform to the rules of her house and saying your prayers was one of those rules. Another rule that was severely dealt with when it was not adhered to was the rule that no lying would be tolerated. Her philosophy was, "If you lie, you will steal. If you steal, you would kill." This brings me to my next antic.

In the spring, it was our tradition to go to Fairmount Park with as many empty jugs as we were able to carry and fill them with spring water. Many of the neighborhood families shared in the same practice. We would often share a ride with some of the neighbors to the park. One of the neighborhood's kids, Lorna was not one of my favorite people. I disliked her because she always had something smart to say. Lorna went with us to the park that day to get spring water. All the kids were filling their bottles while the adults were sitting down enjoying the cool spring air.

Lorna, of course was her usual smart mouthed self. I don't even remember what she said that particular day. I do recall that her words made me so angry, that before I knew it I had slapped her hard across the face. She ran crying to my Grandma telling that I had slapped her. My Grandma sent for me and when I went to her she asked, "Kelsey, Lorna said you slapped her in the face, did you do that?"

I vehemently denied the accusation. Grandma made it very clear to me that if she found out that I was lying to her, there would be serious consequences as she despised a liar. I assured her that I was not lying and Grandma let me off the hook, believing I was telling the truth.

Later that evening, while we were outside playing and Grandma was in the house, Lorna approached me again and as usual she had something smart to say. That's when I pointed my finger at her and yelled out, "that's why I slapped your face earlier today, because of your smart mouth." Immediately, to my surprise I heard Grandma's voice from the 2nd floor window of the house, "Kelsey, come here," she called in her most stern voice. I knew what was coming next.

Grandma gave me a stern lecture and then instructed me to go to the back yard and choose my own switch and the switch had better be to her liking. If it was inadequate, she would go and choose one and I know her switch of choice would not be in my favor.

I came back with an acceptable switch and when I turned the switch over to her she directed me to sit down. When I was seated, crying and pleading for mercy; I felt the switch connect with my legs and thighs as it stung me repeatedly. I knew I was wrong. I had gotten what was due to me, as I had been forewarned of the consequences if I was found to be a liar and I was, by my own admission. The pain of that thrashing lingered with me for several days.

Chapter 7

Dippin Snuff

Grandma Roxie was my Grandmother on my Mother's side. I spent quite a bit of time with her as well. She had a three story house on Webber Street, across from the funeral director's parking garage. She spent most days sitting by the window dippin snuff and using a coffee can to spit in every so often. Grandma was diabetic and could be found early every morning sitting in the dining room injecting herself in the thigh with her daily dosage of insulin. Afterwards, she would begin making a huge and heavy breakfast of gravy smothered fried chicken, grits, eggs and large homemade biscuits. I was never able to eat even half of what was served on my plate. It was way too much food for me.

At six years old, I was the designated dishwasher on these visits. After breakfast, Grandma would fill a bucket with cold water, (there was no running hot water) and then heat it on the stove. When the water was hot, she would pour it into the sink and then mix it with just enough cold water so that my hands could stand it and then set out a bar of brown lye soap. The dirty dishes were scrapped and stacked in preparation for washing. I was not quite tall enough to reach the sink adequately, so a stool was provided for me to stand on. It seemed like I would take forever to complete this chore and I was always glad when the laborious task was finally over. Afterwards, Grandma would have me to snap fresh green beans whenever we were going to have them with the dinner meal.

Unlike my Grandmother Chris' house that was always filled with children, my Grandma Roxie's house was the exact opposite. I was the only child on that side of the family that visited her, known to me at the time.

Grandma Roxie had a mysterious past, to say the least. In later years I would hear stories of her showing up at family events drunk with no underwear on. My Mother, her twin brother Eddie and a great Uncle, (Grandma Roxie's brother) were all we knew of on that side of the family until one day a young man showed up at the door claiming to be her son. That's when we found out that Grandma Roxie had three more children from a previous marriage or still existing marriage (I never knew which).

These children unknown to my Mother or her twin brother, all lived in Detroit, Michigan. Those family members consisted of a great aunt, named Dolly, Aunt Eartha, Uncle Shayne and Uncle Chuckie. Aunt Eartha had a daughter who was about nine or ten years older than I named Madelyn and the next summer my mom and I would have an opportunity to travel by train to meet and spend time with them.

I never knew the details of how Grandma ended up in Philadelphia, Pennsylvania from Detroit, Michigan or who the father of her twins were. By the time I was born, the only Grandfather figure I knew was Mr. Don. He and Grandma Roxie lived together until Grandma passed away when I was 16. I never saw him again after Grandma died. Mr. Don was a quiet man. I don't recall anything he said as he was a man of very few words.

Kelsey from Pain to Triumph

I never heard him raise his voice or recall seeing a smile on his face, but he was nevertheless a peaceful man. He rose early each day and went about doing his chores. When he was finished, he took his place in the chair, facing Grandma at the window opposite her. There they sat, day after day looking out of the window, Mr. Don dozing off from time to time and Grandma spitting snuff juice in the coffee can beside her. I never heard a cross word between them. I never experienced any excitement at any time in that household, (until I brought excitement). It was otherwise utter boredom for me.

One day after sitting at the window most of the morning and afternoon, Grandma got up and went to the kitchen to begin preparing the evening meal.

Mr. Don had assumed the position and was quietly snoring in his chair. While Grandma was in the kitchen on that particular day, I decided to pretend to be her. I sat in her big overstuffed comfy chair by the window and watched as people passed by and children played. I watched as funeral cars went in and out of the parking garage across the street. Then my eyes fell on the small can of snuff on the little table next to the window. I picked up the silver can, removed the lid and took a big piece of snuff, stuck it under my tongue like I had seen Grandma do and held it there as it mixed with my own saliva. Periodically, I would pick up the old coffee can and spit the brown liquid into it.

I repeated this process until Grandma called me and Mr. Don for dinner. Mr. Don got up first and shuffled his way into the dining room. I got up next, but as soon as I stood up the room began to spin around me and my stomach began to churn.

I took a few steps and suddenly I was overtaken by a very sick feeling. I vomited all over the living room floor repeatedly until nothing was left in me to come up but bile. Mr. Don and Grandma came hustling into the living room to see what had taken place. They were both aghast to see the mess that had to be cleaned up. Grandma got a cold damp washcloth to wipe my face and pressed it against my forehead. I was sent to bed and eventually, fell asleep after my stomach settled down.

I awoke to the sound of Mommy's voice and I could hear them downstairs talking about the day's events. Grandma figured out that I had been dippin snuff from her can as the odor of snuff was very strong and poignant. Mr. Don cleaned up the big mess I had made.

Mom came upstairs to wake me and found me already awake with a sheepish look on my face. She asked me if I had dipped snuff from Grandma's can and I admitted that I had done the naughty deed. I was not punished as they all felt that the sickness that I endured as a result of my actions was punishment enough. Mom took me home and prepared some soup for me but I could not eat a thing as the remnants of queasiness had not entirely left me. I went to bed that night vowing within myself to never go near a snuff can again and to this day, I never have.

Matthew 11:28-30 (NLT)

"...Come to me, all of you who are weary and carry heavy burdens, and I will give you rest. Take my yoke upon you. Let me teach you, because I am humble and gentle at heart, and you will find rest for your souls. For my yoke is easy to bear, and the burden I give you is light."

What a marvelous invitation from Jesus who never fails, always delivers and always keeps his word. Who among us that carry heavy burdens would not want to exchange them for a much lighter load? Psalms 105:8 says that he keeps his commitments forever. As we become emotionally tired of carrying the burdens of our past, we can find rest in his care.

Being yoked together with him keeps his investment in us from being compromised. There are limitations on the level of damage that can be done by others in our life. God's divine purpose for each of us has a covering of protection that cannot be penetrated by life's circumstances.

One thing I have learned, my past is past. It has no bearing on my future. It is my choice to leave it behind me where it belongs and focus on the path that God has placed before me. I choose not to waste my energy grieving over a history that cannot be changed. It was what it was. Nevertheless, I have the joy in knowing that it is not today what it was in my yesterday.

Ponder this: God's created universal solar system defies the law of gravity. He carries the weight of the planets, the sky, the stars, the sun and the moon, lest they come crashing to earth's floor. I am reminded of a song we sang when I was a little girl, "He's got the whole world in his hands." A God who successfully carries the weight of the universe in the palm of his hands, how much more can he carry the burdens of your soul that scream out for rest and relief?

The Burden of Childhood Baggage

Chapter 8

Trouble in the Camp

That spring, Mommy bought me a beautiful suit for Easter. It was purple iridescent and I loved it. Purple is my favorite color and I was so excited that I could hardly wait to wear it. As a matter of fact, I didn't wait. Mom put me to bed the night before Easter. Once I was asleep, she left the apartment. Daddy was not home and I was left alone. I awoke the next morning very early and went through the house looking for some sign of Mommy or Daddy and neither parent was at home. I quickly washed up, got dressed in my new Easter suit and left the apartment. It was the custom of that time to parade yourself around to all of the neighbor's houses that lived on your block, showing off your Easter outfit. As I recall this incident I began to realize how potentially dangerous and risky that whole situation was and how it could have been a very different outcome.

As I walked out into the dawn of the day, the cool crisp air rushed to meet me. I didn't care if I was a little cold, I wasn't about to cover up my beautiful outfit with that spring coat Mommy bought me. My Easter suit was a sassy little jacket with three sparkly little buttons in the shape of a flower and a matching box pleated skirt. I loved how the light danced off of the different iridescent hues of color, illuminating shades of purples, grays and greens. I couldn't wait to show it off. I began going from house to house waking up the neighbors to show them my Easter outfit. They all answered their doors sleepy eyed looking at me like I had two heads and they all asked, "Kelsey what are you doing here this time of morning and where is your Mother?" I told each one that I had come to show off my new outfit and I didn't know where Mom was. I then ran next door to Mom's best friend's apartment and rang three doorbells before I was buzzed in.

I could hear the sound of the Blues playing on the phonograph as well as loud voices all talking and laughing in the background. I had to knock on the door several times and after what seemed like an eternity, a man unfamiliar to me finally opened the door. He stood there with a glass of brown liquid in one hand and holding the door with the other hand. He had a cigarette dangling from the side of his mouth. I darted passed him into the living room where I heard all the loud laughter. The stench of alcohol and chitterlings, along with different body odors and cigarette smoke all mingled together, invaded my nostrils.

There was a crowd of people, all talking and laughing loudly about something. Some were standing and some sitting around the room and there was Mommy, stretched out in the middle of the floor. There was one man standing over her, talking and laughing loudly as he seemed to be telling a funny story. Mom was laughing hysterically, her head was thrown back and her whole body seemed to shake as tears of joy rolled down her face. As she wiped the tears from her glazed eyes, her focus finally settled on me and suddenly her smiling face froze. Instantly, her eyebrows knit together as her laughter ceased and a frown took its place. "Kelsey, what are you doing here?" "I came to show my Easter outfit, I said." Mom turned her body to a crawling position as she got up on all fours, the man that stood over her reached down to help her to her feet. "Let's go," she said as she took my hand firmly and marched me from the room toward the front door and out of the apartment. Mommy took me straight home and told me to take the suit off and get back into bed. She said it was too early for me to be up. I cried as I started to take the suit off. Mom hung it up as I crawled back into bed, heartbroken and bawling my eyes out, I finally fell into a deep sleep.

When I awoke again, Mom was lying next to me. Daddy still was not home. This was my first indication that there was trouble in the camp. Dad always came home but after that day his presence was sporadic. Mommy didn't talk about it but shortly thereafter, I was introduced to Sandy. She was to be my very own babysitter and I was glad that I was going to have someone there with me as Mommy began going out often and so did Daddy. They just were not going out with each other. When they were home together, which was not often; I would hear arguing in the next room. Daddy was constantly packing his clothes and threatening to leave and Mommy didn't seem to put up much of an argument to keep him there.

I guess he had hoped that packing would be a sign of permanent separation that would cause Mommy to beg him to stay, but she never did. It always ended with him making love to her and her trying unsuccessfully to ward off his advances.

Eventually, Daddy did make good on his threat and actually left home. Mommy never spoke a word against him to me and never talked to me about why he was no longer living with us. She continued going out and got Sandy to watch me whenever she did.

Once while Sandy was watching me, her boyfriend showed up at the door inebriated. She let him in but asked him to leave shortly afterward as his behavior, was let us say, 'in poor taste.' He would not budge and Sandy went to the kitchen to get a butcher knife in hopes that the knife would strongly encourage him to leave. When he refused Sandy's pleas to go home, she took the knife and hit him on the back of the hand with the blade. She seemed completely surprised when blood began to gush out and splattered all over the floor and over his shirt.

Sandy's eyes got big as saucers and she jumped up and ran in the bathroom and locked the door, leaving me in the living room with her drunken boyfriend.

After his many pleas to get Sandy to come out of the bathroom, he finally wrapped his arm in a towel that Sandy had thrown out of the bathroom door before immediately locking the door back. The towel quickly soaked with blood and he finally decided to leave and go to the hospital to seek medical attention.

When Mom came home, Sandy was straight with her and told her everything that happened. (Apparently, she told some other people as well and the news spread like wildfire throughout the neighborhood). Daddy was hearing different things regarding my care from the neighborhood gossipers.

A few days later, I awoke one morning and after hearing no sounds, I got out of the bed and began going through the apartment calling and then later crying out for Mommy but my cries were met with silence.

Mommy was nowhere to be found. It was a Saturday morning and I waited a while hoping that Mommy had just run to the store and would return soon. After what seemed like an eternity, I became hungry and decided to fix myself something to eat. I went to the ice box (back then, there was no refrigerator instead there was a large appliance box that was not powered electrically but rather had a large block of ice inserted on the top shelf which was used to keep food items cold. When the ice melted you got the ice man to bring another block of ice and place it on the top shelf of the ice box), there I found a package of open bacon and took it out. I wasn't quite tall enough to see over the top of the stove and so I pulled a chair up to the stove, turned it on and began to place strips of bacon on the grill insert in the middle of the stove top. Suddenly, I heard a key turning in the lock on the front door and a familiar whistle that was always accompanied by my Daddy's entrance. I left the bacon sizzling and quickly got down from the chair. Running into my Daddy's arms screaming, "Daddy, Daddy." He picked me up and hugged me as he walked to the kitchen. Spotting the unattended bacon, he put me down and asked, "Where is your Mother?" I shrugged my shoulders and said, "I don't know." Daddy finished cooking me breakfast and after eating ravenously, he ran my bath water and told me to take my bath and get dressed. Afterward, Daddy took me over to Grandma Roxie's house.

After spending the weekend with Grandma Roxie, Mom came to pick me up and I saw that she had a terrible black eye that was blood red on the inside and black and blue on the outer perimeters. I remember having a very sad reaction to that observation as I knew somehow that my Daddy was responsible for it.

Mom never said anything to me about it but I could tell that she was also saddened by this form of physical abuse. I had not known my Daddy was capable of such a thing as I had never seen him put his hands on my Mother at any time before that incident occurred.

Chapter 9

Emotional Trauma

Mrs. India, the elderly lady that lived in the front apartment who warmed my hands and gave me cookies and milk, passed away. All the neighborhood kids loved Mrs. India. She pierced the ears of every girl in the neighborhood, including mine. She had lived in that building on the first floor front apartment for many years. Mrs. India's funeral would be the first funeral I had every attended, and I was not prepared for the stiff mannequin like appearance that I saw when I peered into the casket. I literally jumped back in shock and fear.

That night after the funeral was over, Mommy brought me home and after putting me to bed (I slept in her bed since Daddy was no longer living at home) she told me she was going out for awhile. I was horrified that she was about to leave me alone after such a traumatizing experience at the funeral. I cried profusely and begged her not to go, telling her I was afraid and thought Mrs. India would come back from the dead and get me. She said "Kelsey, it's the living you need to fear, not the dead. The dead can't hurt you." I didn't believe her. My tears flowed all the more as I was sure that Mrs. India would appear when Mommy left and carry me away with her.

Mommy finally relented somewhat and called someone to come and stay with me while she was out. However, she was going to leave before the sitter came and I was in deep anguish over the 30 minute wait I would have to endure before the sitter arrived.

I began that night sleeping with the covers tightly drawn over my head and continued to do so each night for many years to come. Whenever I would start to feel at ease again about going to sleep without the covers pulled tightly over my head, there would be another funeral that I would be forced to attend and the cycle of fear would begin all over again.

Soon after Mrs. India's death, Mommy was getting ready to go out, yet again. She said to me, "Kelsey, your Father is coming over tonight, if he asks you do you want to go live with your Aunt Lee and Uncle J.T., say, 'no.'"

I told her okay that I would. But secretly I hoped that Daddy was not going to ask me that question. I knew it would be impossible for me to say no to Daddy even though I truly did not want to go. In retrospect, thinking back to this change, I was now able to understand how people could sustain some aspect of abuse and still remain in relationship with the abuser.

In spite of all that they go through, they remain unconditionally committed. I am by no means condoning such behavior. I'm just saying there is no rhyme or reason to their commitment; it's just a commitment without a cause.

Daddy did come that night. I was glad to see him as I had not seen him much since he left home. He asked me if I wanted to go live with Aunt Lee and I said, "Yes," when I really didn't want to leave my Mommy in spite of all the trauma and drama I had been exposed to as a result of living with her.

Kelsey from Pain to Triumph

I just wasn't able to say no to him. I was heartbroken as he packed my clothes and we left the apartment for the last time.

Chapter 10

Late Foundational Training

Aunt Lee and Uncle J.T. were expecting me. I was able to discern right away that my brother Tony, who had lived with them several years now had been trained to refer to Aunt Lee as "Mommy" and Uncle J.T. as "Pop Pop." I understood it as they had been raising him and he really knew them and related to them more as parents then he did our own parents. Well, I made up my mind right off that to me, they would always be "Aunt Lee and Uncle J.T." Unlike Tony, for the past seven years I had lived with my parents and knew them and related to them as my parents and had no intention of calling my Aunt and Uncle anything other than exactly who they were, (Aunt Lee and Uncle J.T.).

Looking back now, I can say that I was angry at the turn of events in my life. I was probably most angry with myself than I was with anyone else. After all I had been given a choice regarding my living arrangements and my choice was not predicated on truth but on the inability to stand up to my Daddy and respond to him honestly. Actually, I had some fear of him. Although I loved him dearly, I had seen evidence of his wrath (even though it had not been directed toward me) and I never wanted to be on the receiving end of it, so I made a life changing choice. A choice that I thought would please him based on what I perceived he wanted to hear.

Although Daddy visited us at Aunt Lee's often in the beginning, Mommy didn't visit very much at all. I missed her so much that my heart literally ached for her.

I remember calling her on the telephone and she would allow me to do all the talking. She had little to say to me in return. At the time, I took that as a form of rejection. Later, upon re-evaluation I understood it to be a sign of both hurt and betrayal, more than likely due to my decision to say "yes" to living with my Father's sister.

Things started off a little rough from the beginning, as I had a fear of the dark and often thought I saw shadows in the room or the shadow of someone sitting in the chair across the room. I would cry out in those times and Aunt Lee would come into the room to see what was troubling me. I would tell her that I woke up and thought I saw the shadow of a man sitting in the chair across the room. She would say, "Kelsey nobody is in that chair." Nevertheless, she agreed to leave the hall light on to calm my fears.

Aunt Lee, unlike my parents, lived in a house in a quiet neighborhood and not an apartment. As a matter of fact, from that time forward I would never live in an apartment again until I reached early adulthood, living on my own. My cousin Sherrie, who is more like a sister to me to this day, was a young teenager at the time and still lived at home. She and I always had chores to do but my brother Tony and my cousin Lenny (Sherrie's older brother) had Aunt Lee twisted around their fingers. Aunt Lee always favored the boys and it was clear they could pretty much do as they pleased. They were exempt from chores and never did any wrong in her eyes.

Shortly after my arrival, my grammar was deeply scrutinized and I was corrected pretty much every time I opened my mouth. I was never permitted to say "yeah" and was told constantly to say "yes," not "yeah."

The constant grammar and manners corrections drove me bananas. But now I understand that unlearning something that you have said or done or not said or done since you were old enough to speak takes time and consistency of practice. It's a process of the mind that requires erasing the old and reprogramming the new. It's not easy, but it can be done.

Uncle J.T. was a man of simple taste. His idea of an enjoyable, relaxing evening took place only on the weekend, usually Saturday night. He would sit in his special chair by the front door with his feet propped up on the hassock, smoking one of his favorite Phillies cigars and listening to his favorite records.

Glen Miller, Count Basie, Tommy Dorsey, Ella Fitzgerald and the like was his favorite genre of music. He loved to immerse himself in it as time permitted. On occasion, he substituted his music for another form of pleasure. He would indulge himself in a planned Saturday night card game with his favorite cronies around the dining room table. During the week he was very organized and structured, never deviating from his normal routine or schedule.

Each evening when Uncle J.T. came from work, Aunt Lee would fill him in on the events of the day as he sat at the kitchen table ravenously wolfing down his dinner.

Uncle J.T. often worked late and Aunt Lee, me and Tony would eat without him. His plate would be made, wrapped in foil and set over a pot of water that had just been boiled and then the heat reduced to low and eventually turned off. (There were no microwave ovens at that time).

By the time he got home, his plate was still hot and just before eating he would stand over the kitchen sink filling and drinking water from a quart sized jar. He would refill the bottle and drink deeply again until he had consumed a half gallon of water.

He would then turn his attention to the top of the stove where he found and removed his plate from the pan of hot water. He would remove the foil that covered his plate and then sit down to eat.

Uncle J.T. said little as he inhaled his food. He would always be extremely thirsty and famished at night as he was a truck driver and spent little time eating or drinking throughout the day. He was a man of few words but when he spoke it was usually a profound statement. He had gone to college for two years before he married Aunt Lee. However, due to family financial responsibilities; he was never able to go back to complete his degree. It was very clear to me and Tony that education was extremely important to him.

Every Friday night after he had satisfied his palate with food and quenched his thirst with water, Uncle J.T. would call me and Tony to the kitchen table where we were asked to recite the time table we were given to study at the beginning of the week. This process began the first school year I lived with them and continued throughout my five year stay.

By the time I was in the third grade, I knew all my time tables 1 through 12. This would prove to be a huge asset to me. Once that was accomplished, we would be responsible to learn other important aspects of school work. One project was given each week to study throughout the week. I would come home and change out of my school clothes and complete my chores for that day. The remainder of the time before dinner would be spent with the school project that Uncle J.T. had given us during the week. Friday nights we were always tested on the contents of the project given at the beginning of each week.

Uncle J.T. offered stern encouragement in this area with his weapon of choice, which was the extra wide belt that he put over his knee each time we came to the kitchen to recite the week's study material. He rarely had to use the belt which was nick named, "Uncle Tom." However, just the mere appearance of that belt was enough to ensure that I did my best to please him by learning those things that would come to serve me well throughout my life time.

I was secretly grateful and appreciative for his contribution to the educational portion of my life, even though I disagreed with the methodology used. It made me strive to please him in this area as it seemed to be the only part of me that was good, (according to them). It was one of the few things that I received praise for, a praise that I craved. They both told me often that I had a brain, that I was smart. This kind of praise came throughout the duration of my stay in their household.

I had not been in my Aunt and Uncle's care long before Aunt Lee had my cousin Sherrie to ask me if I would call her mommy instead of Aunt Lee.

It was not something I felt comfortable doing, and I continued to call her Aunt Lee in spite of her request that I call her mommy. After all I had a Mother and did not see the necessity to call anyone else by that title. Aunt Lee began to label me as a child who was stubborn and defiant and this label would be spoken over me for the entire five year duration of my time in that household. I sensed a bit of hostility towards me as a result of my decision to continue calling her Aunt Lee.

Aunt Lee worked part time as a housekeeper for a couple who were both doctors. I always thought that she secretly coveted having a housekeeper of her own but the household budget was not able to support such an expense. However, she had my cousin Sherrie and I do all of the household chores and she used us in this manner to her fullest advantage.

Cleaning would be a very large part of my life in those years. I strongly related to the story of Cinderella as I was taught proper cleaning methods and was expected to put them into practice at every opportunity. I had only one chore when I lived with my parents and that chore was to wash the dishes.

It was a chore that I begged my Mother for months to allow me to do before my wish was granted. At Aunt Lee's I was taught how to iron (this included bra straps and Uncle J.T.'s boxer shorts, as well as Aunt Lee's night gowns. In addition, I was taught to iron sheets, pillow cases, as well as towels and wash clothes.

These pieces were called 'flat pieces,' (which in my mind, ironing these particular pieces was ludicrous but it was not within my power or control to change this practice). It was not long before I was ironing all the clothes for the entire household most of the afternoon on Saturdays after I finished completing my other Saturday chores. I was trained to hang clean, wet clothes on the clothes line outside in the yard. (Even though we had a dryer, it seemed that we rarely used it).

Saturday mornings were set aside to clean my bedroom, to include wiping down baseboards and window sills and organizing my closet. Cleaning the family bathroom was also included in Saturday chores. For the five year duration of my stay with my Aunt and Uncle, I would perform these tasks routinely in addition to cleaning the kitchen every night. The chores required detailed precision to carry them out and was met with a white glove test inspection upon completion.

I was used to washing the dishes but after moving with Aunt Lee I soon discovered that cleaning the kitchen and washing the dishes entailed two completely different criteria. The criteria for cleaning the kitchen meant that after the leftover food was stored in containers and put in the refrigerator, the silverware was gathered together and the glassware was collected and placed together. Dishes were scraped of food remnants, stacked on top of each other and the pots and pans were placed together on the kitchen counter.

Hot sudsy water was run in the sink and you began the washing process with the glassware first followed by silverware and then dishes. Pots and pans were scoured last with a Brillo soap pad and cleanser, inside and out. The stove always had a coffee pot on it and at the end of the day it was part of my kitchen cleanup duties to take the coffee pot apart, empty the coffee grinds and wash the coffee pot in preparation for the next day's use.

The eyes of the stove and its surrounding surfaces also were expected to be cleaned as well as wiping off the kitchen table, place mats and all counter top surfaces to include wiping any food stains off the cabinets and refrigerator door.

The garbage was taken out to the backyard and dumped into a garbage bin that was kept near the gate and picked up by the garbage collectors weekly.

Afterward, the kitchen floor had to be cleaned. Using a mop to mop the floors was not permitted. A rubber pad was provided to protect your knees and you were given a scrub brush and a bucket of hot water with pine sol.

You first put the kitchen chairs upside down on top of the table, then swept and scrubbed the floor. After you scrubbed and wiped up the floor with a soft clean cloth, you then poured out that bucket of water, filled the bucket with fresh hot water and then you wiped the floor again with the clear water to remove any residue of soap.

When the floor was dry, the chairs were taken down from the table top and placed underneath the table. This was a long process and took about two hours nightly and woe be unto you if you forgot to perform any of the tasks described!

Chapter 11

Midnight Madness

On many occasions, I suffered the agony of being awakened from a deep sleep during the night long after the house was quiet and everyone was in bed asleep for the night. During these times, I would find Aunt Lee at the foot of my bed screaming to the top of her lungs about something that I was not quite able to discern. I was a deep sleeper and the premature awakening always found me incoherent and disoriented for the first few minutes or so until I was able to collect my thoughts enough to figure out what was happening and why Aunt Lee was at the foot of the bed ranting and raving about one thing or another.

One particular occasion I remembered by the time I was lucid enough to comprehend the seriousness of the matter I started to cry and began to ask her over and over what she said. It was already too late as it took me too long to get my bearings and she was already headed for the staircase to go downstairs and get 'mini tails' in order to bring me back to full clarity and reality. Mini tails was the name of a concoction made from a plastic clothes line that Aunt Lee had cut into about five or six strips and then tied the strips together to create a flogging device of sorts. This homemade apparatus proved to be a very effective and persuasive tool used in the assistance of bringing one back to their senses expeditiously.

My crime, (I found out after the beating) was that clothing items had fallen down on the closet floor and I had failed to notice and pick them up. This was a scenario that would rear its ugly head from time to time along with other scenarios.

After I was sufficiently flogged, I would then have to correct the error, (which was made worse as the remaining closet hangers were also stripped of their garments and all clothing thrown on the bed in her rage). Before I saw the back of my eye lids again in the escape of sleep, all clothes would have to be re-hung neatly on each hanger and placed back in its proper place in the closet.

Aunt Lee was a tough task master. She would prove to be relentless and unwavering in her training methods. I remember thinking to myself how similar Aunt Lee's behavior was to the actress that played the role of Joan Crawford in the movie, Mommy Dearest. I remember how I felt after seeing that movie. It invoked a deep sadness in me and I was very surprised to discover that I was not alone. There were others who had suffered a similar fate. Some were upper class, some middle class, and some lower class. There were some rich, some poor, some of one nationality and some of another. I discovered that abuse was not limited to a particular class, ethnicity or financial stature of people. It was a disease, bigger than I could have ever imagined.

Chapter 12

No Rhyme or Reason

Sometimes the abuse was unfounded and unprovoked. Those times hurt me the most, as they were more difficult to justify in my mind. Two incidents in particular, stand out to me.

Once we were going to have a play in school and I had been selected to be one of the cast members. My teacher, Mr. Crawford thought I would do well in one of the parts. I told him, I could not stay after school to practice for the play. Mr. Crawford told me not to worry. He would write me a note to take home that would account for the time I would be late.

I got home an hour late. For a change I thought that I had a legitimate reason and I would have one of those very rare days that I did not get a beating after school. I felt carefree as I went home that afternoon. My relief was short lived as I neglected to factor in that Mr. Crawford's hand writing looked like that of a child. It was much like chicken scratch and did not give Aunt Lee any other impression except that I had one of my friends to pen the note. I got one of the worst beatings that day that I had ever had. Every time I would say, my teacher wrote the note I got another lick with mini tails and was called a liar. Aunt Lee said she was not going to stop beating me until I admitted that a friend wrote the note and not the teacher. I cried fiercely, not so much because of the physical pain inflicted but more because I had to lie to stop the beating. I was angry, frustrated and filled with a sense of hopelessness.

After I conceded that a friend wrote the note, my confession was then met with a barrage of licks and her words of self-assurance that she knew I had lied about the teacher being the writer of the note. That night, I cried myself to sleep.

One day, when I came straight home from school (for a change), Aunt Lee was waiting for me. She was screaming about a box of candy that she had hidden and I was being accused (as I often was) of rambling through her things, finding the candy and eating it. I tried to tell her that I didn't eat the candy and I didn't even know she had the candy.

Of course, mini tails was summoned and every time I said I did not eat the candy she would hit me with mini tails. This was another one of those occasions when I had to lie and say I ate the candy in order to stop the beating, which of course brought on a barrage of licks designed to satisfy the crime's punishment. I felt angry and helpless, crying out to God to get me out of this situation.

That night when Uncle J.T. came from work, Aunt Lee told him how I had rambled through her things, found and ate her candy and then lied continuously about the incident until she beat me into telling the truth. She triumphantly showed Uncle the half eaten box of candy and to her amazement he said, "Lee I ate that candy." Aunt Lee's mouth dropped open and she said, "But she admitted to taking it." Uncle J.T. looked at her and said, "I would have said I did it too if you were wailing on my backside." They both laughed at her blunder.

Uncle J.T. rarely involved himself in the actual beating process of the day to day issues and other disciplinary aspects of our child rearing. I suspect, somehow he knew that the beatings were being sufficiently covered.

I waited expectantly for an apology. I finally felt I would be vindicated. However, the apology was not forthcoming and to add insult to injury, Aunt Lee said, "I may not always be right, but I am never wrong. That beating was for something you did that I did not catch you in." What!!! Are you kidding me right now, I remember thinking to myself. Nope, she was not kidding. Wow, I felt hurt once again and defeated. That night, I cried out to God to remove me from the situation.

One morning I was preparing for school, I washed up, brushed my teeth and went back to my room to decide what to wear. I only had four school outfits and spent a lot of time trying to figure out how to mix and match them from day to day so that it didn't look like I only had four school outfits. I finally decided on what I would wear and proceeded to dress and comb my hair. When I was finished I pulled the mirrored closet doors opened as they faced each other so that I could see the front and back of myself in the mirror. Satisfied that this was the best that I could do, I grabbed my school books and started downstairs where Aunt Lee usually waited with breakfast.

Only this time when I approached the kitchen she was sitting in one of the kitchen chairs with an angry scowl on her face and mini tails in her hands. My eyes widened as a morning beating was rare and most unexpected. She jumped up from the chair and started toward me.

I dropped my books on the floor, made an about face and the chase began. She chased me up the stairs and I was able to make it to my bedroom, jump in my bed and pull the covers of protection over me. The covers were viciously snatched from my body and a severe beating began. She usually talked to me during the beating. Example: didn't I tell you not to…, (as you were simultaneously given a lick for each word). Only this time, she said nothing. She just stood there with lips pierced angrily together and swinging mini tails with all her might.

I kept screaming, "What did I do; what did I do?" No answer came and when the beating was over, she turned and walked back downstairs, without a single word.

I lay there crying and wondering what in the world I had done to deserve such a life? To this day I was never told what that beating was for and it haunted me afterward for many years. Right now as I write these things that I had previously pushed in the deepest archives of my mind until now, I find myself whispering, why? Why? I will probably never know on this side of heaven. I do have the consolation in knowing that God's word says, we see through a glass darkly but when we come face to face with him there will be an opportunity for clear answers regarding all the things we wondered 'why' about in our lifetime.

Chapter 13

Basement "Time Out"

I began to rebel more and more and as a means of compensation, so to speak I decided I might as well indulge to the fullest in those small pleasures I allowed myself. This way, I would at least feel some measure of vindication for the injustice of many of my severe punishments. I remained true to the character of the terms 'stubborn' and 'defiant' that were spoken over me and at every opportunity I failed to come straight home, using that time to wallow in the freedom of being away from all that I had come to despise. I felt unloved, unwanted and barely tolerated.

New methods were introduced by Aunt Lee in an attempt to keep me in check. One that comes to mind is the basement. It was a dark and scary dungeon like place that I would be sent to wait for the beating. Sometime it would be several hours between the time I was sent to the basement and the time the beating would commence. Ironically enough, it would be the place that I spent many hours in prayer, asking God to grant me relief from my adversity.

Aunt Lee normally did not believe in beating clothes, they cost too much to replace. The rule was that you striped down to your underwear and stood in the corner of the basement shivering with fear of the unknown. When will she come? What sound is that I hear? Is it the scurrying of a mouse?

Aunt Lee was well aware of my fear of the dark, so of course during those times of prayer and meditation in the basement, I was confined to the dark.

I was instructed to stand until she turned the light on and came down the stairs with mini tails and the small radio from the kitchen that was used to drown out my screams. The basement, though narrow ran the full length of the house. In the beginning, Aunt Lee was able to get in one lick before I could run to the other end with her close on my heels. She was in her 40's and out of shape and got winded easily. At the other end, another lick was administered and the chase would ensue again. Afterward she would be totally out of breath and spent from the high impact aerobic exercise the beating caused.

Soon Aunt Lee realized that these beatings were wearing her out. A new plan had to be put into practice. A wooden chair was placed at the front of the basement near the radio and a rope was used to tie me to the chair so that she no longer had to use precious energy to chase me up and down the basement. When the beating was over and the rope untied, I would be led upstairs to the kitchen wear the usual ritual of dressing my wounds took place and she would always say, "I beat you because I love you."

Occasionally, the trip to the basement would not result in a flogging, but would yield another form of punishment. The place where I stood was right below the kitchen and I could smell the dinner meal.

Kelsey from Pain to Triumph

Aunt Lee was a great cook and my mouth watered for her well prepared and delicious meals. However, dinner was not provided on these occasions and at times she would go to bed and forget that I was down there.

Sherrie would be left to clean the kitchen up and once her task was complete, she would sneak down the basement stairs and bring me a sandwich. I was grateful to her for her compassion.

She would even go upstairs to Aunt Lee's bedroom door and knock until she was given permission to come in. Sherrie would say, "Mom did you forget Kelsey is still in the basement?" Half asleep she would mutter "I forgot, tell her to come upstairs and go to bed."

Many nights I lie in bed with silent tears rolling down my face, asking God to remove me from my situation, but my prayers were met with silence as it was not yet the fullness of time.

Chapter 14

Motherless Child

In spite of all that I had been through, time was not standing still and I had miraculously lived to see my 11th birthday. Aunt Lee was still working, and Tony and I would go to Sherrie's house. Sherrie was now married and had a beautiful little baby girl named Jacklene. Whenever the baby would be brought to Aunt Lee's for a visit, I would bathe her, dress her up and comb her hair. She always looked so adorable and after the 'Kelsey treatment,' I would bring her downstairs and parade her before Aunt Lee for her approval.

Jacklene was the apple of Aunt Lee's eye and received many accolades of praise from her just because she was a beautiful baby and her first grandchild. This beautiful little girl would be instrumental in helping me to get my mind off my troubles. She was a joy to be around and very accommodating, patiently allowing me to enjoy playing dress up with her as she fulfilled the role of a real live baby doll.

Sherrie lived within walking distance of our house in a cute little basement apartment. Although it would flood all the time whenever there was a hard rain, at least it was her very own.

I envied her and always dreamed of the day when I would be able to leave Aunt Lee's as well and be on my own. Sherrie would give us a snack after school and we would do our homework there and then walk home once Aunt Lee called to say she was home from work.

One evening about a week before Christmas, my cousin Lenny came to get me and Tony from Sherrie's. It was later than the time we were usually sent home and this particular night Sherrie fed us dinner as she sometimes did when Aunt Lee was going to be delayed at work. I remember thinking to myself how it seemed strange as he had never come to get us before. We were always permitted to walk home by ourselves. Lenny then called me and Tony into the living room and asked us to sit down. He started talking about my Mom and how she had been sick lately and had spent the past two weeks in the hospital, (which I already knew as Aunt Lee had gone to visit her and reported back that she was getting some test done).

I wanted to go see her as well but Aunt Lee said that Mom didn't want us to see her like that. I figured we would get a chance to visit with her as we did on rare occasions, once she came home from the hospital.

Only Lenny told us that Mom wasn't coming home. His words hit me like a ton of bricks and I felt my heart sink into the pit of my stomach. It was not making sense to me as he seemed to be rambling on and on and suddenly just blurted out that Mommy had passed away at 10:00 a.m. that morning.

I kept waiting for him to say that he was only kidding as Lenny was known for being a big prankster. Throughout the remainder of that evening Tony never said a word. He seemed to process the news differently than I did. Not uncaringly, but not emotionally either.

Kelsey from Pain to Triumph

We left Sherrie's and on the long silent walk home the tears began to fall freely down my face. It was starting to sink in that I would never see Mommy alive again. I would never kiss her or be held by her again. She would never again be able to proudly show me off to her friends as she did on our most recent visit, pulling my sweater down tightly over my chest and teasing me about the two little bumps, almost the size of golf balls that had suddenly appeared on my chest in confirmation that training bras were in my near future and that I was approaching young womanhood.

No more would I watch her as she stood in the mirror wetting her brush and then brushing her hair into a pony tail with a full bang across her forehead. She had beautiful hair and even though she would sometimes have it permed and curled with a hot curling iron, I liked the water and grease ponytail and bangs best. Never again would I see that smile that showed a gap between her two front teeth. A gap that I had inherited and was very proud that when it was widely displayed in a big smile, people thought I looked exactly like her.

When we got home, Aunt Lee was sitting in the living room talking to Uncle J.T. She greeted us just as she did every day. We were told to get ready for bed. Just like that, no hugs or kisses, no words regarding the day's most devastating event. Nothing that would remotely suggest that she even knew what had taken place.

Once again I lay awake with tears running into my ears. I remember thinking, why didn't Aunt Lee tell us? Why were there no consoling words of comfort? Why was Lenny called to be the bearer of such news? He lived in another part of town not even close to Aunt Lee's or Sherrie's. Yet he was given the task of bad news bearer.

Even at age 11, it seemed strange and bazaar to me as if Aunt Lee didn't know how to comfort us with hugs and whispers of assurance that everything would be alright.

An even more bazaar event was that morning in school we watched a film on agriculture. I remember during the film and unrelated to the film a very sad feeling began to overtake me. I began to cry uncontrollably and could not stop. The teacher tapped me and beckoned me to go outside of the classroom with her. I noticed the clock on the wall read 10:00 a.m. I got up from my seat and followed her into the hall. She asked me why I was crying but I couldn't tell her because I didn't know why. I just felt very, very sad. I was told to get a drink of water and go to the bathroom and wipe my face.

The funeral and burial took place on Christmas Eve. Mom lay lifeless in the casket. Aunt Lee asked me when it was our turn to view my Mother's body, "do you want to kiss your Mother goodbye?" I loved Mommy so much that my chest ached, but I still had a deep rooted fear of the dead and that fear robbed me of that last act of love and affection. I hated myself because I couldn't say goodbye in that way, after all she was my Mother and I loved her dearly.

Mommy was 31 years old when she passed away. I was told she was poisoned. It would be years later before I would discover that 'poison' was actually a disease called End Stage Renal Failure. This disease is caused by a nonfunctioning or low functioning kidney allowing toxic waste to build up in the body with no means of escape. It was a time before treatments such as dialysis or kidney transplants were discovered.

For many years, I kept hoping that some kind of terrible mistake had been made and it really was not her lying in that casket and one day the doorbell would ring and I would run to open it and she would be standing there with a big grin on her face. But years would go by and what I hoped for would never come to be.

My Daddy spent the night with us at Aunt Lee's but he was feeling pretty sick and he spent Christmas day lying around on the sofa. That Christmas we got more toys then we had ever gotten on Christmas before.

I suppose Aunt Lee was trying to show us some kind of compassion and love in the only way she knew how. Instead of it being a happy day, it was one of the saddest times in my life, knowing that Mommy would never be able to experience new changes that would occur in my body. She would never be there to share with me that special bond that I wanted us to share. We would never have those teenage mother and daughter talks. She would have been so proud, watching me evolve into a young woman. Life was cut off, swiftly, with little warning. One day she was fine and two weeks later, she was gone. I felt cheated, how can this be? Again I found myself asking the Lord, 'why' but no clear answer manifested.

Chapter 15

Out of Control

I had only one pleasure that I was allowed and that was riding my bicycle on Saturday afternoon after all of my chores were done. My bike allowed me the freedom to go places that I would not otherwise have been able to travel undetected.

I would ride and ride all over the West side of town without fear of repercussion. It was the only real joy I had. I would be gone for hours just riding and stopping along the way for a chat if I saw someone along my journey that I knew.

One Saturday as I was preparing to go for a ride, I brought my bike outside and put the kick stand down. Aunt Lee called me from the door as I was about to leave, "Kelsey, before you go, can you go upstairs and see if I left my wallet on the dresser. I thought I brought it down when I came downstairs but I don't see it." (She never knew where she put her wallet and either Tony or me always had to go looking for it for her).

I turned to Tony and said, "Watch my bike until I come back." He said, "Okay." He was sitting on his own bike when I entered the house. I found Aunt Lee's wallet pretty quickly as I knew all the places where she would absent mindedly put it down. After giving her the wallet, I told her I was leaving and she hollered, "You had better be back in this house by six." "Okay," I called over my shoulder as I walked out the door.

When I approached the front steps, I noticed that my brother, his bike and my bike were not in front of the door where I had left them. I started down the steps as I looked up and down the block but I saw no sign of Tony or the bikes. I was about to run around the corner where he often went riding with his friends when Tony comes riding around the corner on his bike. I look at him with eyebrows raised and I said, "Where is my bike?" Tony squeezes his brakes as he looks around with a dumbfounded look on his face. He scratches his head and swallows hard as he looks at me and says, "I don't know. This big boy came around the corner and told me that my friend Rodney was looking for me, and I just went around the corner for a minute to see what he wanted but I didn't see him so I came right back." He started to open his mouth to speak again but before he could get another word out, I punched him hard in the belly. I knew that he had been conned and someone had taken my bike and had taken away the only freedom that I had in the process.

I started crying and went running in the house to tell Aunt Lee. She came to the door and yelled out, "Get in here." He tried to explain but his words were met with a slap across the face. Aunt Lee went to get Mini tails out of the draw and Tony ran upstairs crying. Aunt Lee ran up behind him and commenced to wailing on his tail like there was no tomorrow. Tony hardly ever got a beating, but this time he was shown no mercy.

The next day, Tony was let outside to ride his bike again. I was devastated as I was now left without a bike and without any freedom at all. My free time was now spent on the porch or sitting on the steps outside. I thought to myself that things could not be worse. I hated my life now more than ever.

During this time the abuse began to spiral more and more out of control and as the abuse was, so was my stubborn and defiant behavior more and more out of control. Looking back, I now know that I had a crude and elementary dysfunctional strategy of sorts to put more and more pressure of poor behavior into the equation with the hope that it would become too overwhelming for Aunt Lee and Uncle J.T. Ultimately, bringing about a favorable outcome: An outcome that would yield a result whereby I would be removed from that home and placed somewhere more to my liking. The truth was, I hated it there and was desperate for a change that would eliminate the painful abuse from my life.

To some degree, my plan seemed to be working as Aunt Lee was getting pretty fed up with me. Mini tails was now being accompanied by other tools of the trade. Now anger caused Aunt Lee to use whatever tool was at hand. It could be a broom handle, (held baseball bat style), a kitchen pot or the spike heel of one of her shoes, just to name a few.

I always healed physically but my attitude was in line with my emotions and that healing would not come easily. I stayed clear of Aunt Lee as much as possible. When I had to be in her presence I said as little as possible. Of course she noticed and went out of her way to engage me in conversation. I would pretend not to hear her and would continue with what I had to do around the house. This would make her very angry as she knew I heard her. Once during this kind of scenario, she walked up behind me and hit me in the back of the head with a glass baby bottle. "Do you hear me talking to you?"

My anger would swell to the point that I refused to allow tears to overtake me as I thought it gave her some sort of satisfaction. No matter how severe the pain from the abuse, I would scream if the pain was too severe but I purposed in my heart not to shed another tear. I would just stand there and look at her with my lips tightly pierced together and my eyebrows knit closely together.

I could tell that Aunt Lee was growing weary of her inability to break my stubborn and defiant behavior as I not only continued to rebel in coming home late from school, but I began to display poor behavior in other areas as well. She would eventually become exasperated with me and began to talk about seeking outside help that would be instrumental in rehabilitating me.

Around this time I remember being invited to a birthday party. It was going to be on a Saturday night and I badly wanted to go. However, I wanted to somehow break the cycle of being questioned about who the parents were of the person who was having the party, were the parents going to be home during the party, etc., etc. I was rarely given permission to attend such celebrations especially if they took place at night. The ritual was that I must provide the telephone number and address of the party. Aunt Lee would then call the parents of the friend to verify all information regarding the party and if she was satisfied, I would be driven to the party at 8:00 p.m. and picked up at 11:00 p.m.

This time the party was scheduled to begin at 11:00 p.m. I begged to go but Aunt Lee held a firm position about the times I could attend. So I finally had to agree in order to be able to go. I was however able to negotiate being driven and picked up as opposed to walking the three blocks.

I begged and pleaded this point using the argument that it was embarrassing to be the only one driven and picked up and that I would be walking with another friend who was also going (which was not exactly the truth), but I was desperate for some of the normal freedoms that had been withheld from me most of the time. I would have said anything to go to this party and not be driven or picked up. After all, I was not a baby I was almost a teenager. She finally agreed to allow me to walk the distance as long as I walked there and back with my friend. Aunt Lee knew the party was going to be in the neighborhood on Burton Street but I told her I did not know the address and I was only familiar with the house by site. (I didn't want her to change her mind and show up to pick me up and have all the kids laughing at me).

I was anxious and excited. I left the house that evening telling Aunt Lee before I left that I would be meeting my friend Lily at the corner at 7:45 sharp to walk together to the party. Of course, she inspected me as she always did before I left the house. Checking to make sure my under garments looked presentable, (one of her many idiosyncrasies. She was always worried that I would meet with some accident and be taken to the hospital with undergarments on that would be an embarrassment to her). I was never kissed goodbye but instead I would get a mini lecture on proper behavior and reminded of the 11:00 curfew. After the preliminaries were over I rushed out of the house feeling a sense of freedom and anticipation of the evening's events to come.

I walked swiftly toward Burton Street, it was summer and the night air felt good after a hot day. It was still light outside as it got dark around 9:00 this time of the year. I arrived at the party and rang the bell. The birthday girl, Francine opened the door and seemed surprised to see me so early.

"Hi, you're early but I'm glad you're here. I could use a hand blowing up some balloons. My jaws are getting sore."

I was the first one to arrive and that always meant helping out with the last minute party preparations. I began helping blow up balloons and hanging streamers. The party was going to take place in Francine's basement. As we finished putting on the plastic party table cloth on the long folding table and putting out bowls of snacks, Francine said, "by the way, your Aunt called my parents." We both laughed as Francine's parents often called other parents to confirm her story, so she understood and was really cool about it.

The bell started to ring about 10:30 and little by little the other kids started trickling in. Francine's older brother was the DJ and he had already begun to spin the latest rock n roll tunes on the turntable. He had set up a black light and turned off the basement's bright lights for effect. Someone snuck a bottle of vodka in and was emptying it into the punch bowl.

Francine's parents stayed upstairs, and the party was just starting to rock. I looked at my watch and it was 11:05. My heart sank as I was just beginning to enjoy one of the rare occasions of being at a party and actually having a blast. At that point I decided that since I was already late and would be punished even for the slightest delay past 11:00, I might as well throw all caution to the wind and party with wild abandonment. We all had a great time and in spite of the punch being spiked no one got out of hand. My decision to miss curfew, would mark the beginning of a new level of rebellion. The party ended at about 2:00 a.m.

I felt too good to go home and face the music, so to speak. I just didn't feel like getting a beating that night after having such a good time.

I was the last one to leave as I had no clue what I was going to do. Walking down the street I suddenly had the idea to sleep in one of the cars parked along the street. I began to try the handle of different car doors until I found one that opened. I got in the back seat, closed the door and lay down. The alcohol allowed me to block out all thoughts of the consequences of my actions. I would let tomorrow take care of itself. Tonight, I would just bask in the afterglow of the evenings events. Sleep came almost immediately and my next memory was waking up with the day light sun warm on my face and a sick feeling in the pit of my belly just thinking about the beating that lie ahead.

I sat up and thought I had better get out of the car. After all, I had just slept in a car not knowing when the owner may suddenly appear. I looked around and everything was quite. I quickly and quietly exited the car and began to walk down the street. I still was not ready to go home and face the music. I wasn't really sure what to do. I walked around a bit trying to clear my head and trying to decide what to do next. My bladder was full and in need of release. It wasn't long before I decided to go to the police department and tell them I had stayed out all night and was afraid to go home.

I entered the precinct that morning and walked up to the desk sergeant who had his head down writing. Finally, I cleared my throat and he looked up and said, "Can I help you?"

I began telling him my story but the words were not coming out loud enough and he couldn't hear me. "Speak up, young lady." I took a deep breath and began again. "I'm afraid to go home," I said. Then I just blurted out that I had gone to a party the night before and had not been home. The Desk Sergeant asked me to take a seat. He left his desk and went into one of the back offices.

He came out a few minutes later with a lady who came over to me and introduced herself. She said she was a police officer. I asked her if I could use the restroom as I was about to bust. She led me to the ladies room and waited for me outside the door until I was finished. When I came out, she took me into an office and asked me to tell her what happened and I had to tell my story all over again. She listened attentively and then gave me a piece of paper and a pen and told me to write down my name, address and telephone number. She then asked me to follow her. I followed her and she led me to a cell and told me to sit in the cell while she called Aunt Lee. I sat down on the hard cot that was in the cell. It seemed like an eternity passed before the officer came back to the cell to tell me that Aunt Lee was on her way to get me.

When she arrived, I could tell she had been crying. Of course she wanted to know where I had been all night and why I had not come home. I offered no answer but shrugged my shoulders and just sat there with my head down. Aunt Lee started crying. She said, "I just don't know what to do with you anymore." She started going on and on about how she had tried to give me a good home and be a mother to me. The police officer gave her something to sign and we were told we could go. We rode home together in silence and when we arrived, Aunt Lee told me to go upstairs and take a bath.

Afterward she grilled me for over an hour about where I had been, what I had done and why I didn't come home. I was not permitted to say, "I don't know." I was finally told to go to my room. I got into my bed and pulled the covers up over me, waiting for the beating that I fully expected to come.

Time went by and eventually, I could no longer keep vigil. I found myself drifting into a troubled sleep with troubled dreams. I slept a long time and awoke much later in the day. Fear still gripped me. I was hungry but only left my room to quietly tip down the hall to use the bathroom and then return to my room. For a while I could hear voices downstairs but after a time, the house grew silent. A knock came at the bedroom door. I said, "Come in." The door knob turned, the door opened and Sherrie was standing there holding a sandwich and a glass of milk. "I thought you might be hungry. Mommy and J.T. had to go out and she asked me to come over and watch you." I eagerly grabbed the plate and started to wolf down the sandwich. I was starving and so grateful to Sherrie for always looking out for me. "Thanks," I said taking the milk from the side table where she sat it.

Sherrie didn't ask me any questions and I didn't offer any explanations about the night's events. She just sat there on the bed beside me making small talk. I hardly heard a word she said as I was still in a state of apprehension. Wondering when Aunt Lee would suddenly make an appearance with mini tails. The day passed quietly and uneventfully. To my surprise, the beating that I anticipated never came. For the first time, I began to sense calmness within that I had not felt in a very long time. I sensed something different in the air, but was unable to put my finger on what it was.

Romans 5:20 (NLT)

"God's law was given so that all people could see how sinful they were. But as people sinned more and more, God's wonderful grace became more abundant."

The love of God runs so deep that He does not insist on our perfection in order to receive his abundant grace. His love is without conditions. He understands that a lasting change for the better is more likely to take place when we know that we are accepted in the beloved just the way we are. So much so that while we were yet sinners he purchased our freedom with the precious blood of Jesus, His only begotten son.

Beating someone over the head, (literally or figuratively), does not give one the inner pressure or motivation to change. However prayer is an access key that allows the Spirit of God to gently guide and direct us toward change. He knows when the time is right and He knows when our hearts are open and receptive for change. He is patient and waits until the season and the circumstances are perfect to bring about his desired result within us.

We know the areas of our life that harbor sin. We also need to know that without God, we can do nothing. We need not worry excessively about our inability to overcome in some of our weak areas. God's grace is sufficient and His promise to complete the good work he has begun in us until Jesus returns is our guarantee that those areas we struggle in will one day be changed for our good and for his glory.

God Steps in Right on Time

Chapter 16

Defiance at its Peak

All through the week, Aunt Lee said very little to me. She stayed home that week and did not work her part time job. I did notice that she spent an excessive amount of time on the telephone. Calling different agencies trying to get information on how to go about placing me in some type of school or program designed to get me on track in the area of my behavior. I overheard her say that she could no longer cope with me and wanted to know what she needed to do to get some type of help for me through the justice system.

My behavior continued to spiral out of control. I was suspended from school for fighting. I didn't want to tell her because I did not want to reap the consequences that would surely come as it was my third suspension in a Junior High School that had very strict rules. I got up each morning and prepared to go to school as always. I had no idea of what I would do to pass the time until school was out for the day. So I went to school as usual pretending that all was well. I saw another girl of similar behavioral problems who had also been suspended at the time, named Christine who was in the school yard as well. Before the bell rang, we talked about ways we could possibly pass the time. In our finite wisdom, we decided to hang out in the girls' bathroom all day. We were putting on makeup, singing and writing down the words to the latest Smokey Robinson song, "Shop Around" and telling stories.

After several hours had passed, we could hear one of the teacher's just outside the bathroom door. We both quickly gathered up our books and purses and scurried into different stalls in the bathroom.

We had already devised a plan in advance that if a teacher came we would stand on top of a toilet seat inside separate bathroom stalls so that our feet would not be seen and upon quick perusal, it would appear that the bathroom was clear and no students were lagging behind. However, the teacher who entered the bathroom did more than a quick perusal. She actually opened the door to each stall. We were both mortified when the stall door flung open and there we were crouched on top of the toilet seat.

Of course we were questioned as to our names, why we were not in class, who our home room teacher was, etc., etc. Needless to say we were marched to the principal's outer office and after a brief time of waiting, we were called in separately and both expelled permanently for being on the school grounds illegally. Christine's parents were called and the school called Aunt Lee. We had to wait until we were picked up.

I got the beating of my life that day and Aunt Lee did not know what she was going to do with me. After I was home for several days, Aunt Lee was informed of a school in a very seedy part of town called Carson School for Girls. Kids in similar situations had been sent there that were permanently expelled from the school in their jurisdiction and had no place else to go. Aunt Lee did not want to send me there and tried to find another option. But the wheels of justice grind exceedingly slow and she had no other choice but to allow me to be placed there.

I quickly understood why it was called "Carson College, the school of no knowledge" as there was very little curriculum taught there. After roll call the days were spent with various mundane activities, such as straightening and curling our hair.

This is where I would learn how to use a curling iron from the other students. They were mostly in the age category of 13 – 15 years old. I was the only one that was 12. The other students already didn't like me much as I was the new girl and they did not take kindly to the intrusion of new students infiltrating their little clicks. When one of the girls asked me how old I was, I lied as I wanted desperately to fit in. My time at that school was very short lived. Two suspensions would cause me to also be expelled from there as well.

The first suspension occurred when I allowed myself to be strongly encouraged that if I wanted to be a part of the group I needed to do something that would gain me entrance into their click. I was asked by one of the girls if we had any wine at home. I remembered that we did, that I had seen a bottle of wine in the dining room cabinet. I knew that it would be missed if I took it because Aunt Lee and Uncle J.T. were not big drinkers and only consumed alcohol when they had company. Occasionally, Uncle J.T. would have a cold glass of red table wine with his dinner. Nonetheless, I was so desperate to fit in that I decided that I would risk it.

The following day, I got the one bottle of wine that was in the dining room cabinet, placed it in a brown paper bag and put it in my briefcase before I left for school. I felt apprehensive about the whole idea from the start but decided to go through with it. When I arrived at school, I went to the cloak closet and found a little corner where I placed the wine. I let the girls know that I had successfully kept my end of the bargain. Throughout the day, different girls would go to the cloak closet and take a swig or two of the wine. All went well until the end of the day. I somehow did not realize that at the end of each day, the teacher checked the cloak closet.

I never had an opportunity to hide the bottle that just had a small remnant of wine left in it. The teacher checked the closet and there in the corner was the bottle with a small amount of wine left. She demanded to know who it belonged to and we were told that if someone didn't confess, that the entire class would be punished. The girls all pointed to me and said that I had brought it into the class. My first suspension was about to take place after only being at the school a few months.

I dreaded going home that day. The school called Aunt Lee and she was waiting for me when I arrived. I don't have to tell you what took place next. I was sent to the basement to wait until she was ready to give me my punishment. I could hear her coming down the basement stairs and tried to prepare my mind for the beating that was about to take place.

Chapter 17

The Last Straw

The day I returned to school after my three day suspension, I walked into the classroom and all eyes turned to me as one of the girls yelled out, "My girl, 12 years old!" They all laughed. Somehow they had managed to eyeball my records from the teacher's desk no doubt. Scanning her roll book and looking at documents and paper work on the teacher's desk is something they often did whenever the opportunity presented itself, which occurred whenever the teacher was out of the room for a brief time.

They were a crude, rude rowdy bunch of rough necks. Nevertheless, I still tried to fit in. I was able to discern from bits and pieces of conversation that I would over hear from time to time, that the majority of them came from unstable, single parent, lower class backgrounds. I thought the wine incident and ultimate suspension would help me to get into their good graces, but they had learned my real age and knew I had lied to them about being older. So instead of being celebrated as I had hoped, I was barely tolerated.

I sensed something was brewing among them. Some trick, some scheme as they always whispered a lot just before something wild and crazy was about to go down. I found out later in the day that they were planning a fight after school and I was their target. They had carefully chosen one girl who thought of herself as a bully and always boasted about her great fighting skills. She began to instigate the pending act by talking out the side of her neck about what she was going to do to me and how she was going to do it. I had no fear of the girl personally.

My fear was activated by cause and effect. I knew that the school had a strict automatic suspension policy for fighting and I had just come back to school from a three day suspension. I kept my mouth closed and tried to think of a way to escape their ruse. But my trying would be in vain. The school bell sounded as an indication that class was out for the day. "Class," what a joke! I can't remember one single thing that was studied or taught besides learning how to use a hot hair curling iron. Deep down inside I missed learning and the stimulation my mind received when I attended regular Junior High School. I deliberately lingered in the classroom after the other kids disbursed, pretending that I was looking for something. The teacher noticed that I was still there and looked at me with a raised eyebrow. I walked up to her desk, taking a deep breath I began to tell her what the kids had planned for me after school, begging for her help. She just shrugged her shoulders and told me not to engage in fighting but to go straight home. I knew at that point I wasn't getting any help from her. I slowly gathered my things and left the class. As I walked down the hall, the vice principal was standing at the door to her office and I decided on a whim to tell her what was about to take place. I didn't get much help from her either. She basically reminded me of the consequences of being involved in a fight in or around the school area and advised me to steer clear of any such activity.

I left her office as I felt the anger begin to boil inside of me. These people just didn't get it. There was no way I was going to stand there and let that girl hit me without her feeling the full wrath that had been pent up inside of me for five years with no outlet. If she hit me, I planned to do my utmost to kick her black behind!

As I got to the school entrance, I could see a crowd across the street waiting. I walked out and proceeded down the block. I tried to focus on getting to the trolley car as I could see it coming from a distance.

I knew that if I missed this one, not only would that give the gang of roughnecks a chance to catch up to me but I would be suspended again for fighting and I would also be late getting home from school. Neither of these outcomes seemed to be avoidable as I could see the crowd running across the street in my direction.

I set my things down on a bench that was at the trolley stop as I didn't want to be caught off guard with items in my hands. Although I had no intention of throwing the first punch, as soon as the gang caught up to me and began to form a circle around me, the lead bully made her stance and balled up her fist, I clocked her two good, hard swift punches upside her head.

The crowd began to roar, "...get her!" I became like a raging bull as I pounced on her with all the fury that my anger ignited, whoopin' her like she was a stranger. I was angry because I knew the outcome to this unavoidable situation, a situation that I had no control over. I figured, if I had to suffer consequences for an act that I could not evade, I would make her pay and pay dearly for putting me there. I don't recall a single blow from her connecting to me in anyway. I'm sure there must have been some but if there were, I didn't feel them. I was too intent on punishing her for putting me in this predicament. I saw a police car approaching out of the corner of my eye and as they stopped and exited the vehicle, the crowd disbursed and they all ran in different directions. I was left standing there alone huffing and puffing and fighting mad. I had lost all sense of reality and had displayed the same crude rude behavior that I despised in them.

The police asked me what was going on. I explained to them what happened and they escorted me back into the school. Of course, I was suspended again. Aunt Lee was called and told about the fight. She asked to speak to me and they put me on the phone with her. I had to listen to her rant and rave saying, "Kelsey, you are incorrigible, I don't know what I am going to do with you." No one sympathized with me, no one understood that I was placed in a position of fight or flight and I chose to fight. If this made me "incorrigible" then, so be it. I was not sorry one bit! After all I had done my best to avoid the inevitable but it was not to be.

I sat on the trolley car during the long ride home feeling defeated. I won the fight but lost the battle, the battle to come out victorious in the face of adversity and to make matters worse; I had to go home and be subjected to another fight, one that I was not able to win. One where I would be labeled: rebellious, defiant, incorrigible.

I am reminded of what Paul said, "Even when I want to do what is right, I inevitably do what is wrong.... But there is another power within me that is at war with my mind. This power makes me a slave to the sin that is still within me. Oh, what a miserable person I am! Who will free me from this life that is dominated by sin and death?"

Of course Aunt Lee was waiting for me with Minnie Tails. I was led to the basement as usually, told to strip down to my underwear, tied to the chair so that I could not run and beaten as I screamed over and over with each blow. Afterward, the usual ritual took place. I was led upstairs where my wounds were dressed and once again told I was beaten in the name of love. I went to my room afterwards and cried out to God again. "When God, when will I get relief from this painfully insane life?"

I cried myself to sleep and the following morning I awoke to see Aunt Lee standing over me, telling me to start packing my clothes because I would be going to live with my Father. She no longer wanted the responsibility of raising me. I was too this and too that. This time the movement of God could be seen. The fullness of time had come. Change was on the horizon. I silently thanked God for his grace and mercy.

I finished out my suspension time at my Father's house that he shared with his current girl friend who just happened to be the former best friend of my Mother. (That was a bit of information that I had no prior knowledge of as I never went to visit Daddy, he always came to Aunt Lee's to see us). I often wondered if his girlfriend was also his girlfriend before my parents split up or did she more recently become a girlfriend since my Mother's death? That was a question that I would never know the answer to.

I returned to school after my suspension period and to my surprise I was embraced and greeted by the roughnecks with their interpretation of "love." I had tried all I knew to be accepted by them, but that which I avoided the most, was the one thing that gained me access into their click and hence into their good graces.

Since the fight, I got much respect from them during my duration of time at that school, even from the girl that I had just whooped a few days prior. Who knew?

Chapter 18

A time of Transition

I was glad to be with Daddy. That first weekend, we talked a great deal. I had an opportunity to tell him of the many abusive encounters that took place while I was at Aunt Lee's. Daddy was very careful to write every occurrence down in a little black book. I just knew he was going to let Aunt Lee have a piece of his mind. I don't know if he ever said anything to her or not about the abuse. If he did, I never was privileged to receive that information.

I minded my p's and q's while I stayed at Daddy's house. I came straight home from school every day and stayed out of their hair as much as possible. I thought if I was good enough, Daddy would let me stay. However, my time at Daddy's was very short lived and within a few weeks I was taken back to the one place that I dreaded more than any place in the world. I was hurt and confused. I realized at that point that although I knew he loved me, there was no permanent place in his current life for me.

Aunt Lee let me know upon my arrival that I wasn't staying there. She said, "If it's the last thing I do, you are going to be put away." I secretly looked forward to being "put away" as long as it was someplace that utilized a different form of punishment when you messed up. Aunt

Lee and Uncle J.T. sent me to a psychologist to be tested. It was a long day of many tests. I remember one test being a bunch of cards with splatters of ink patterns that required me to tell the psychologist what each card looked like to me. After completion of many test, my scores earned me an overall rating of above average intelligence, confirming that I indeed did have a brain.

Aunt Lee continued her quest to get me placed in a real school. Carson School for Girls was now totally unacceptable. I was even taken to a Youth Behavioral Center in hopes that they would keep me there. The administrators there told Aunt Lee that the children housed at the center were there by a family court judge's orders and she would need to go through the family court system to have me placed. By this time Aunt Lee was quite exasperated as all her efforts to be rid of me seemed to be in vain.

Finally, she had gone through enough red tape to receive a court date in the mail to bring me to family court for a hearing. I was as anxious as she was to have an opportunity for placement somewhere else, anywhere else except her house. Somehow in my mind I perceived that I would be placed in a foster home or girl's home of some sort. The day finally came for our court appearance. When my name was called, we stood before the judge. A stack of papers were given to him to look over and Aunt Lee was asked to tell the judge all of the highlights of my worse moments since I came to live with her. The judge ordered me to the Youth Behavioral Center pending admittance to Falcon Boarding School for Girls.

Just like that I was swept up and taken to the Center by guards. I felt like I was going to jail as I was put in a caged wagon with other youth (many of them were offenders of the law). I thought of myself as only an offender of Aunt Lee and was thrown in with those who were worse then I.

Upon arrival we were all searched from head to toe. Our hair was inspected for lice and we were each given a fresh bar of soap, a towel, a new package of underwear and a blue uniform. We were all led down a narrow hallway. At the end of the hallway benches were flanked on both sides. We were instructed to sit on a bench until our name was called.

I sat and waited until my name was called and then I was led to the bathroom. As I approached the entrance, I was told that I had 15 minutes to wash, dry and get dressed. I washed leisurely as the hot bath felt good to my body. It wasn't long before a knock came on the door and I was told to hurry along.

I knew that I probably should have felt some kind of way about this new and very structured environment, but oddly enough I only felt a sense of relief that I was out of Aunt Lee's house.

There would be many times in the years to come that an adverse situation would give me that same sense of relief that no matter how bad things appeared, it couldn't possibly be as bad as what I had already endured. I was looking ahead to a brighter future. One that although virtually unknown, held the promise of hope and the anticipation and expectation that things were about to get better. Although it looked like I was in a downward spiral at the moment, I perceived that things were actually looking up.

As I reflect on this period of time, revelation came to my mind that God had moved and I was grateful that my prayers were answered. Prayers prayed by a soul that once gave her life to Jesus and was baptized before the age (six) of accountability, now seemingly backslidden, in comparison to the parable of the sower and one who received the seed on stony ground. (Matthew 13:18-23). Although her current life looks as though she has changed her mind about God, God never changes his mind about any of us. A long awaited, desperate prayer was answered. Not because my behavior warranted it, as I can attest that it didn't. It was because of his great love that prevails not based on a good behavior but in spite of a bad one. I began to think back to his promise of a foreknown plan that he already had for me: a plan of prosperity and not of harm, a plan that included hope and a good future. Somehow I knew that this band of time was carved out as the beginning of a preparation for the good future that was to come.

Chapter 19

Holding Pattern

The Youth Behavioral Center was like a holding pattern, a place where you waited for placement into a more permanent environment. Although it was for girls and boys, we never saw or had opportunity to interact with the boys as they were on one side of the building and the girls were on the other side. I would hear whispers though about the few girls who were selected for cafeteria duty and how they managed to steal kisses and Lord knows what else from boys through a kitchen door that connected the two sides of the cafeteria. New girls were never selected for cafeteria duty and my time in the holding pattern was short lived.

On the floor where I was placed, there were six large rooms, three on each side of a long corridor. Each room had four single beds shared by four girls. The girls that I roomed with were nothing like I expected them to be. I thought they would be hardened gangster type criminals but through my eyes, they were all ordinary girls that had come from dysfunctional families and became rebellious just as I had. They were a mixture of different nationalities and cultures. We got along surprisingly well and spent long hours whispering late into the night of the horrors that had brought each of us to this place.

The morning alarm clock was the loud voice of the morning housemother whose high heeled shoes could be heard walking down the corridor each morning opening doors and turning on lights as her thunderous voice called out repeatedly as she opened each room door, "Step lively girls, to your doors for prayer, girls." Her name was Ms. Jackson, but no one called her that. To us she was known as Ms. Step lively. Her routine would usher us into the dawning of each new day.

Ms. Step Lively would lead the prayer as we would stand at the door in our pajamas, holding hands with our eyes closed, (more because we were still sleepy from talking half of the night and less because of the customary practice to bow your head and close your eyes during prayer).

After prayer we would get our tooth brushes and wash cloths and enter the huge bathroom flanked with sinks on one side and toilets on the other side. The so called mirrors that were attached to the walls were made of tin instead of glass and you could barely make out your reflection. This somehow bothered me more than anything else at the center. So much of life was unclear at that time, I wanted to at least be able to see a clear reflection of myself in a real mirror but real mirrors were not permitted and we had to make do with what was provided.

The day was filled with meals, card games, board games and various other activities. Our only chores were to make our beds and keep the bathrooms clean. Most of the girls complained about it but to me these two things were a piece of cake compared to the chores I had to do at Aunt Lee's. Saturday was family visitation day. If you had a visitor, one of the housemothers would come and escort

Kelsey from Pain to Triumph

you to the family visitation room. I had been there several months before I received any visitors. I was surprised when I was told that I had a visitor and even more surprised when I was escorted to the family visitation room and Aunt Lee stood there looking very thin. She was smaller than I had ever seen her before.

For the first time, she hugged me. She had tears in her eyes and appeared very nervous. Although, elegantly dressed she looked ghastly. Her jaws and eyes appeared to be sunken in as if she had not been sleeping well.

She appeared to be a mere shadow of her former self. Always a proud woman, that held her head high, I sensed a decline in her confidence level. She did most of the talking through her tears. Her conversation directed mainly toward why I was there and how she was trying to do all she knew to do to keep me from turning out to be a bum.

I assured her that I was okay. After all I had been through, seeing her looking like that still brought about a feeling of compassion for her within me that I had not known existed.

It seemed like the tables had turned and though my future was uncertain, I was happier than I had been in five years. Yet, she appeared sadder than I had ever seen her in that same five year period of time. When the bell rang to signal that family visiting hour was over, we hugged again as Aunt Lee prepared to leave.

I had turned 12 years of age the previous summer. I had arrived at the center in early fall when the leaves on the trees were just starting to turn. Within that same year on Christmas Eve, I was told to gather my things; that I would be moving that day to Falcon Boarding School for Girls. I had a sense of excitement as I wondered what the school would be like. The trip was several hours by van and there were a few other girls who would be traveling with me to the same school. It crossed my mind during the ride to my new home that for the first time in five years of almost daily beatings, that I had not had a beating in almost four months. For right now, that in itself was enough for me. The future held great promise and I looked forward to it with great expectations. I silently thanked God for answering my prayers. I felt relaxed and at ease as I started to drift off to sleep during the ride.

Chapter 20

Falcon Boarding School for Girls

I awoke from my nap as we were approaching a huge school. It was surrounded by acres of plush land as far as the eye could see. We were definitely in the country, I thought to myself. It was Christmas Eve and this new beginning was my early Christmas gift. I could hear church bells in the distance chiming a hymn. "Oh come, oh come Emmanuel and ransom captive Israel. That mourns in lonely exile here. Until the Son of God appear. Rejoice! Rejoice! Emmanuel. Shall come to you, O Israel."

As I look back on that day, I now think of that scene as an introduction to a new beginning. I can imagine the writer of this hymn, announcing to the world how Israel, like sheep, had wandered away from God. Held prisoner by their sin, they longed for the promised Savior who would restore their relationship with the Father by making "his son an offering for sin", thus making "intercession for the transgressors." (Isaiah 53:6, 12) The Savior would pay the ransom that was owed and would lead the captives into the presence of God.

The hymn writer tells Israel to rejoice because Emmanuel is this Savior. Emmanuel means "God with us." God Himself would be their Savior just as He had always been in times past. God is not unconcerned or unaware of their troubles. No, He loves those who are lost and comes to save them personally. We are to rejoice as well. Christ's sacrifice was so great that it couldn't be limited to just Israel.

He is "salvation to the ends of the earth." (Isaiah 49:6) He is my salvation and your salvation and the salvation of any who call upon His name. (Romans 10:12-13). How fitting was that hymn. Although, I did not know it at the time, I now understand why I felt so at ease, so hopeful, so expectant of how this new living arrangement would change my life, and it did not disappoint me.

We finally reached the path to the front gate. The driver stopped at the entrance and punched in a code that was attached to an iron upright panel.

The gate began to slowly open and the van began to enter and it started down the path that was flanked by many large two storied, grey stone cottages. In the distance I was able to see the Church steeple and the bell that chimed that beautiful hymn of hope, assurance and salvation. Each grey stone cottage had a large plaque outside that boasted the name of that cottage. At the very end of the path was a cottage called Martha Washington.

This would be the cottage where each of us would reside for the next three months. At that time we would have become acclimated enough to the routine of the school to be permanently placed in one of the other permanent cottages. As we were ushered off the bus and into the cottage, we were introduced to the housemother and each of us was led to our own individual rooms where we had a twin bed, a dresser, a closet and a chair. Each room had a window.

I was elated and quickly began to put my clothing away in the dresser drawer and in the closet. The clothing was provided for me by the school. There were uniforms for school with black and white saddle oxfords, underwear and socks. There were also jeans and tee shirts and sneakers for all other occasions and a few sets of skirts, blouses and a few dresses for chapel. On the bed was a handbook with a typed welcome letter.

We were given a group tour of the cottage that included the laundry room, the kitchen, dining room, living room and bathrooms. There was also a room called the clothing closet where freshly washed and ironed skirts and blouses as well as jeans and tee shirts and the uniforms for school were kept.

After the tour, we were told to return to our rooms and study the handbook until the dinner bell at which time we would come to the dining room for our first dinner meal. We each stood behind our chairs as the housemother rendered the blessing for the food, a resounding "Amen" was said simultaneously by all as chairs were pulled out and seats were filled by the girls at each dining room round table.

The girls at the table where I was seated were friendlier than I had expected and immediately began to introduce themselves and fill me in on what to expect at the house as well as the daily routine of the school overall as we consumed our meal. The house chores were many and once a month the duties rotated and a schedule was posted at the end of each month to inform each girl of what her chore would consist of the following month.

There was much to do in order to keep a cottage of that magnitude properly maintained and organized so that everything ran smoothly. We worked in teams: the kitchen help consisted of dishwashers, pots and pan washers, daily potato peelers, cooks, waitresses that set all the dining room tables for each meal as well as bussing the tables and sweeping and mopping the dining room floor after each meal. There were also laundry room duties and floor buffing duties and so forth and so on.

Each girl either went to school in the morning and did house chores in the afternoon or went to school in the afternoon and did house chores in the morning. I enjoyed the team work efforts as it helped to build a strong camaraderie among us. At the end of the day after all chores were completed, we showered and spent time doing our homework in our rooms each evening. Lights were out at 9:00 and the housemother went to each girl's room to say goodnight and ensure each girl was safely in place. After room check, an alarm was set to alert the housemother in the event of someone coming out of their room during the night. The alarm box would let the housemother know whose door had opened so that she would know who to check on to ensure all was well. Occasionally, someone would come out of their room to complain of a headache, stomach ache or other miner discomfort. We would be given the appropriate medication and sent back to our assigned room for a good night's rest.

That first night I remember lying there after all was quiet and the lights were out, having such a strong feeling of gratitude for where God had brought me from as I drifted off into a tranquil sleep.

Chapter 21

Acclimation Process

The school also boasted land that had a sizeable orchard filled with fruit trees which were maintained and harvested by hired hands. In addition to many acres of land that had been cultivated and seeded for a sizeable vegetable harvest. During the summer months the vegetable gardens would be weeded during the early morning hours as well as harvested when all was ripe. The school also ate the fruits and vegetables from the land.

This feat was also a chore performed by way of rotation by a team of girls. After working the field in the morning, that team would shower, have lunch and spend the afternoon with their assigned schoolhouse curriculum. I recall this being my chore assignment. At the time, unknown to me, I would later discover how fitting it was that I would have that chore as my first assignment. Years later I became known by my friends and co-workers as one who had a green thumb with the ability to bring a half dead plant back to life and would often be asked to do so with good success.

Surprisingly enough it was school that motivated me in a positive direction the most. I would learn the skill of key boarding which through much daily practice led to a better than average typing speed as well as the enhancement of other secretarial attributes. We were all very competitive when it came to trying to outdo each other with error free speed increase. The school had one of the first models of the very first IBM card punch machine designed for school training and corporate use. I was fascinated by its features and spent many hours learning and mastering its functions.

I learned many things during that time both technical and agricultural. We also had a music class that I thoroughly enjoyed.

In addition, the choir practice that we received in the music class during the week, prepared those of us who were selected to sing in the choir for the morning Chapel service each Sunday. Each of these various skills served me well and has played a large and very significant roll throughout my lifetime. The time passed swiftly and before long it was time for me to select and be moved to a permanent cottage on campus.

We were given three choices of cottages that we felt would be a good fit. I submitted my three choices but secretly, would have been happy to move to anyone of them. Several weeks later I was called into the office, informed that I had been selected to move to Lancaster cottage and that I should pack my things as I would be leaving the temporary cottage on the following day. Lancaster Cottage was my first choice. I was excited and spent much of that evening, packing and saying my good byes to the girls that I had shared many hours with during the last few months. I was also looking ahead expectantly to a new cottage, a new room and new alliances.

Chapter 22

Two Year Turn Around

Two leaders from the Lancaster Cottage were sent to pick me up on foot. They had a large wagon which they pulled behind them. The wagon was used to put my boxes of clothing, school books and various other items that I had managed to accumulate over the past three months. Although one person would have been sufficient to escort me to my new living quarters, there was a campus rule that no one was permitted to walk alone on campus. Therefore two escorts were sent for me.

When they arrived, I was ready to go and hugged all the girls that I had spent the last three months getting to know. Finally, I turned to the escorts and smiling I said, "Hi I'm Kelsey." They each introduced themselves as they started to pick up my boxes and load them on the wagon. "I'm Abbey said the tall girl with the grey eyes. "They call me Dee," said the other girl as she held her hand out for me to shake, "that's short for D'andrea." In a few minutes the wagon was fully loaded. I turned once more as we began walking down the path and gave one last wave to those who were looking out of the window waving back at me.

Lancaster cottage was equivalent to about three long blocks from Logan cottage. So it was not long before we arrived at the stately grey stone faced cottage. Once inside, the cottage had a striking resemblance to the Logan Cottage. I realized that all of the cottages must look pretty much the same on the inside. I was shown to my room which was at the top of a huge staircase and down a long hall on the right. The boxes were brought upstairs by the escorts and once they were set in a corner of the room, I was given a tour and introduced to the other girls. There were three corridors, each one had ten rooms. The cottage was filled to capacity as I was the 28th girl residing in Lancaster house. The two remaining rooms were set aside for the housemother and the cook.

The chores were set up exactly as they were in the temporary house. There were some privileges to being in permanent housing that were not available to temporary housing recipients. One of those privileges was the monthly appointment to the on sight beauty parlor. Another was the Friday night movies at the on sight theater.

Many of the girls complained about the chores, but I was alright with them as the team concept made the chores fun. Whether we were buffing halls with buffing cloths under our feet as we shuffled back and forth to the music, which made the floors shine like a new penny or weeding fields on a cool summer morning, there was something about working together that made it fun for me. Even on rainy days the field workers would be given a substitute indoor task of sanding the wooden dining room chairs, first with course, then with medium and last with fine sandpaper until they looked like new.

They were then shellacked and left to dry. In later years I have done several small projects bringing life back to old worn furniture using the methods that I had been trained to use until those furniture pieces looked brand new again. I excelled in every area. I felt good about my progress. There were a few bumps along the way but when those bumps came, I was corrected. That meant, a Friday night movie privilege would be lost or for more severe punishments, there were cottages strictly set aside for a short stint of solitude. It was a strict rule of the school that fighting or confrontational behavior would result in serious consequences. Those consequences entailed a time away from your normal everyday surroundings and duties.

Miss Larson, the head supervisor on campus in charge of implementing all disciplinary action would be called. She would come to the cottage and talk to you to get your side of the story first. However, the end result was almost always accompanied by a short period of time in a separate cottage where you would not receive any of the privileges normally granted to you. Instead you would be placed in a room that had a bed, and a small bookcase filled with books. This period of time could last anywhere from a weekend to a full week, depending on what Miss Larson deemed appropriate based on your offense. I had only one occasion to be a guest at the cottage of solitude.

It all began when the monthly chore rotation was posted on the bulletin board. As it was my custom, I went to see what chore I would be tasked with for the month and who my chore teammate would be. A quick perusal of the monthly chore posting showed to my dismay, that I had been paired with Jamie for kitchen duty. She was a student that had a reputation for being a bully. I had not previously been paired with her for any chores, yet I was not looking forward to it. I started to protest about the chore rotation, but decided against it.

The morning kitchen duty was done after breakfast. The responsibility of kitchen help was that one person would wash all pots and pans used in preparing the meal and the other person would peel, wash and cut up potatoes for the noon and supper meals. Each week we were supposed to change places and whoever washed pots the previous week would peel potatoes the following week. Jamie hated washing pots and after breakfast she quickly went to the kitchen and began peeling potatoes for the day.

I came in the kitchen and started washing the pots. After the week was over and a new week began, Jamie came in the kitchen and started peeling potatoes. After two weeks of this scenario I decided that the third week, I would not wash pots. We both entered the kitchen at the same time and while donning our aprons Jamie said, "I'm peeling potatoes, you wash the pots." I could feel my temperature begin to rise and before I knew it, I was in her face screaming to the top of my lungs that I was not washing pots. Jamie threatened to kick my behind if I didn't wash the pots. I was still screaming that I wasn't washing pots and she could do whatever the (blank) she wanted, except peel potatoes.

Jamie appeared shocked at my outburst and so was everyone else that came running in the kitchen to see what all the commotion was about. They all stood with their mouths wide open, including the cook, Miss Dalton. Jamie retreated to her side of the double sided metal sink and began washing pots. I started peeling the potatoes on the opposite side of the same metal sink. When the chores were completed, we were both told to go to our respective rooms, that Miss Larson had been called and would be paying both of us a visit.

Jamie began to argue with the cook saying, "what for? I ain't do nothin." I said nothing and instead took off my apron and went to my room without a word. While waiting, I decided that I wasn't going to tell my side of the story. I was still angry and didn't believe for a minute that telling my side would make a bit of difference regarding the outcome. I figured since I allowed some choice wording to escape my lips, I was doomed anyway.

Kelsey from Pain to Triumph

Thirty minutes later Miss Larson was knocking on my room door. I opened the door and she came in. She greeted me cordially and in her soft but firm voice she asked what happened. I kept my lips tightly pierced together and uttered no sound. She tried to engage me in conversation by saying she had already talked to Jamie, but I stood my ground refusing to speak. She finally said that she thought I needed some time away from the cottage to think about what happened and to allow me some quiet time to adjust my attitude. I stood up and walked out the door ahead of her, thinking to myself, *Maybe I do.*

Not only was the time of solitude affective but it was much less painless than methods of punishment experienced in times past. In addition, the solitude that comes with this time out method allows you time to rest, reflect and restore a sense of calm and self-control to your being. During this time of meditation and isolation the Lord spoke to me, (not audibly, but through the heightened sensitivity at the very core of my being). It was in these times that I felt myself being gently stirred into alignment as he began to mold and shape me on the Potter's wheel into the vessel I would ultimately become.

It was a method of operation that did not cause anger or rebellion to bubble up in me as past methods of guidance and discipline had created.

While doing internet research of the school many years later, I came across a place for those who viewed the site and made various comments in the section for reviews. In looking at various comments I was amazed that one comment in particular written by a woman who had at one point been a student at the school described it by saying "I was there for a year and I hated that hell hole." My perspective of the school was that of a glass half full and from her view, it was a perspective of a glass half empty. What made it a "hell hole" for her I wondered? Perhaps due to a decade that had elapsed from the time I was there, until the time of her arrival a drastic change had taken place? Perhaps demonic forces of evil had been dispatched and covered the region years after my departure? Perhaps her time prior to her stay at the school was a frying pan experience, so to speak and the school represented for her a leap from that frying pan into the fire? My experience, on the other hand was the exact opposite.

I can only speculate as to the many possibilities of how one person can perceive a situation as an imposed place of bondage while another perceived it as a place of deliverance.

That which was preparation for my future brought haunting degradation for someone else. How strange I thought, that two people can be at the same place with the same opportunities and both have a completely different experience. Yet, it seemed to have done precisely that. In my life, this system of rehabilitation did what it was designed to do. I had settled into the routine of the day to day chores, classes and activities. The time passed and changes in my attitude and thought processes took place.

Chapter 23

The Next Level of Transition

Two years had passed since my arrival at school. There were many things that I enjoyed. The competitive nature of those classes that I had exceptional skills in, such as the typing class, encouraged me to work with utter abandon to be at the top of my game in speed and error free work. There were others who had developed nicely in this particular course and I found it both challenging and rewarding to try to outdo them at every opportunity.

Outside of the curriculum, I also enjoyed movie night every Friday and the long three mile walks after church every Sunday. Singing songs as we walked along the path with huge shaded trees on either side, and afterwards there would be quiet time in our rooms. I would take a nap during quiet time and as Sunday was visitor's day, on occasion Aunt Lee, Uncle J.T. and my brother Tony would come to visit. They always brought a huge picnic basket full of goodies and they would stay a few hours asking questions about the school. I didn't share a lot with them as I somehow felt that if Aunt Lee knew how much I was enjoying it, she would find a way to ruin it. I was vague when they asked me questions. Mostly, giving yes or no answers and not expounding on anything.

One weekend, Daddy came to visit me. But unlike Aunt Lee he didn't grill me with so many questions. I'm sure he could tell that I was happy and being treated well. He shared with me all that was going on in the lives of all my old friends. We had a great visit and he promised to come back again (although he never did). I didn't hold it against him though, I knew he didn't have a car of his own and he had to borrow a car to come see me.

Most girls stay at the school approximately two to three years. Since I had just passed the two year mark, I began to feel anxious about my future. I knew one thing for sure and that was very clear to me. I would never go back to Aunt Lee's again, ever.

Once a month, each of us would be scheduled to see one of the Social Workers in the Administration Building. It would be a fairly short visit, about 30 minutes or so. During the visit to her office she would ask how things were going, how I was getting along. If everything was okay, so forth and so on. This particular visit, she began talking about Aunt Lee and how she was preparing for and looking forward to my return home in the near future. I abruptly blurted out, "I'm never going back there." The Social Worker seemed surprised at my outburst and wanted to know why. She kept saying, "That's your home." I frowned and said, "No, it isn't." I guess she was at a loss for words as we spent the remaining 20 minutes in silence. I didn't get the impression that she had ever encountered a student that did not want to go home. I believe she was at a loss of what to say or even do regarding my outburst.

I heard girls talking about going home all the time. They would often count down the months and then the weeks and the days until their time was up. Not me though,

Kelsey from Pain to Triumph

I never thought about it and I wasn't about to start thinking about it now. The only sound in the room was the sound of the clock ticking. When our time was up, she scheduled an appointment for me to see her again the following week. I left the office and walked back to the cottage with two other girls. I was silently talking to God, "Lord you can't send me back there, not now, not ever." I felt tears welling up in my eyes. I had to swallow hard a few times to keep them from falling. I didn't want the others to see me cry.

The week went by slowly. I had decided to tell the Social Worker on my next visit, something I had heard that home is where the heart is. My heart was definitely, not there. I was anxious to see her again as our previous conversation yielded no resolution, and I had not slept well the whole week thinking about what I could tell her that would change her mind about sending me back there.

I had made the mistake once before of not speaking my true feelings regarding this same issue, and I was not about to let someone decide my fate again without allowing my voice to be heard regarding the matter. The difference was, now I was soon to be 15 years old. I was no longer seven and no longer afraid to speak up for myself.

My next scheduled visit to the Social Worker went very different than what I had expected. I had spent much time throughout the week prepping myself in defense of my position. I arrived ten minutes early, but she was with another student so I had to wait. I spent the time silently talking to God in my mind, (a practice I had begun doing whenever I needed to talk to Him and others were around. It served me well as I knew that He could read my thoughts and they couldn't). Shortly thereafter, the Social Worker's door opened and I recognized a girl from one of the other cottages come out. The Social Worker was behind her and she stuck her head out, "Kelsey, you can come on in." I stood and took a deep breath and walked into her office.

She sat down behind her desk, and I sat in the chair in front of her desk. "How are you?" "Okay," I said.

I spoke to your Aunt Lee, she was surprised that you did not want to go back home. You do know that if you don't go back, when your time is up in a few months, you will have to go to a group home? Are you willing to do that?

I asked her what a group home was like. She handed me a brochure for a group home that the school had worked with from time to time. It was instrumental in housing young teenagers that had no place to go, in order to provide a final transition into young adulthood as they were prepared for college or a job and a place of their own. We went over the basics about the group home and I was excited but was unwilling to show my excitement, so I kept a calm exterior while my insides were rejoicing.

I was all prepared for a debate to secure my future and before I got to say a single word, an equitable solution had been found that I was very excited and pleased with. We spent the entire time talking about it and I left her office feeling like a huge weight had been lifted from my shoulders. She let me take the brochure with me and told me as I was leaving that she would schedule an interview for me to meet with the head of the organization that governed the group home and make preparations to take me into the city for that meeting.

I must have read that brochure from cover to cover 20 times or more. I hoped that the upcoming meeting would go well as the managing agent for the group home had to approve me before I could be accepted. For the first time in 26 months I began to talk about leaving and looked forward to my next transitional move with great expectation.

Chapter 24

Meet and Greet

The day came when the school Social Worker and I would go into the city to meet Mrs. Johnson, head of the group home. I didn't feel well that day as it was that time of the month for me. My whole body ached from my head to my toes. But I didn't mention anything to the Social Worker about not feeling well. I didn't want her to reschedule the trip as I had been looking forward to it for a month and was very anxious about the meeting in general.

I had no clue exactly what Mrs. Johnson would be looking for or what questions she would ask, so I didn't know how to prepare for it. Also, this would only be my second time leaving the school grounds in 27 months and going into the city again brought about a sense of excitement and nostalgia all by itself.

The first time I was off campus was when one of the housemother's who took a special liking to me and another student named Arlene invited us for a day trip to the city that included lunch and my first time going to see a popular theatrical play called Oliver Twist. As a matter of fact, it was my first time going to see a play. Cultural outings of this magnitude happened rarely and only through school trips. The housemother concluded that outing by gifting us with the album of all the songs from that play. Arlene and I listened to that album on a daily basis in our free time. We played it over and over as we sang the lyrics, learning every single word to every single song. Just the thought of this delightful memory warms my heart to this day. It confirms that the things we do in our lives to bless others, means something and often leaves an indelible imprint and impact that is never forgotten. Often the giver of the blessing views the blessing as some little thing. Not realizing that the receiver holds it very dear.

After a long drive the Social Worker and I arrived at the group home agency. I was surprised that the office space was in a residential area on the West side of town. It was sandwiched between two houses on either side of it.

My mouth was dry and my insides were jittery. We exited the vehicle and walked up to the door and the Social Worker rang the doorbell. A lady answered the door and the Social Worker greeted her warmly as she handed the lady a card and introduced herself. The lady smiled and asked us to come in and have a seat and she would let Mrs. Johnson know that we were here.

As we sat, I felt a wave of nausea come over me and I closed my eyes and swallowed hard, fighting back the feeling. The Social Worker asked me if I was alright and I shook my head yes. I could hear someone on the other side of the office door talking on the phone in a rather loud voice. Her manner was very stern and authoritative. After several minutes, the door to the inner office opened and a beautiful smiling lady walked briskly toward us with her hand extended. She said, "Hi I'm Pat Johnson." We both stood up as she shook each of our hands in turn. Mrs. Johnson asked me to wait while she talked to the Social Worker in her office and that she would call me in shortly.

The Social Worker and Mrs. Johnson talked in her office about 15 minutes. When the Social Worker came out, she asked me to go in. I stood up, my legs felt like rubber and the palms of my hands were sweating. The outcome of this meeting would determine my fate. I wanted to make a good impression. When I entered the office, I was asked to have a seat across from her. To my surprise she had a file in front of her that she was looking through that had my name on the cover. My mind started to race, I hoped that there was nothing in it that would discredit me. I had a few scrapes here and there at the school but nothing that I considered to be detrimental.

Mrs. Johnson finally looked up from the folder with that smile on her face. She began to talk about the group home which was actually located in a brownstone not far from the office. She said I would be going there for a tour of the house where I would also be served lunch by their cook. I started to relax a little. After she gave me a brief overview of the group home and what the girls were like, she turned her attention back to the folder.

Her smile was fading as she began talking about my past behavior before coming to the school as well as my behavior since I had been at the school. We first talked about my school performance since I had been at Falcon as well as my performance in house chores and my ability to get along with other students. She made it abundantly clear that behavioral problems would not be tolerated if I was to be accepted at the group home. I was able to assure her that I would not disappoint her if she gave me the chance. At the close of the interview Mrs. Johnson told me that during the next 30 days my behavior would be evaluated and she would be receiving a report from the school based on that evaluation. She would make her decision at that time. It was a challenge that I was fully up to and knew I could meet.

Mrs. Johnson, the Social Worker and I left the office to go to the brownstone where I would be living if all went well. It was a short drive away and we went in Mrs. Johnson's car. The Social Worker sat in the front with her and I sat in the back seat. They made small talk on the way and I was silently taking in my surroundings. We arrived and the brownstone was impressive, I must say. It was a corner three story property.

We rang the doorbell and were met at the front door by a housemother who greeted us and introduced herself as Mrs. Reedy. We were led to the kitchen and there we were introduced to the cook as she was preparing lunch for us.

I was still cramping pretty bad and as soon as we sat down in the dining room and the grace was said over the meal by the housemother, a wave of nausea hit me again. I asked to be excused to the restroom and unfortunately it was right off of the dining room area. Luckily the sink was next to the commode as I began to release all that was in my body from both ends. I could hear them talking in the next room. Mrs. Johnson credited herself with the condition of my nervous stomach, telling the others that she may have been a bit harsh with me during our meeting. After my body was void of all that was inside, I rinsed my mouth out and blew my nose. I then washed my hands and returned to the dining room.

By this time, they were halfway finished with the meal and as wonderful as the meal looked (fried chicken, mashed potatoes and gravy, green beans and biscuits and warm apple pie with ice cream) I was not able to eat very much. Mrs. Johnson asked me if I was okay and I explained to her that this was my time of the month and I was indeed not feeling very well. After lunch, the cook began to clear away the table and Mrs. Reedy rose and invited me to follow her for a tour of the house. The brownstone was very large and spacious. The main floor consisted of: the entry way, a large living room area, a hallway that had an office to the right of it that led into the dining room and kitchen. A door off the dining room led to a large finished basement.

Upstairs on the second level was four very spacious bedrooms and a very large bathroom. One of the bedrooms was set aside for the housemother. Each bedroom had two beds and two closets and was nicely furnished.

The third level had three large bedrooms and one large bathroom. I was impressed and looked forward to what God was about to do in my future.

Exodus 33:19 (KJV)

"And he said, I will make all my goodness pass before thee, and I will proclaim the name of the Lord before thee; and will be gracious to whom I will be gracious, and will shew mercy on whom I will shew mercy."

There is a song whose lyrics proclaim, "As I look back over my life, and I think things all over, I can truly say, that I've been blessed, I've got a testimony." A testimony is a solemn declaration of truth, spoken in order to persuade a deliberating body of people. Its purpose is to gain the affections of the hearer upon careful consideration. Not of what we have done but of how we made it over by way of the invisible hand of God working on our behalf. His word tells us that his plan for our lives is fail proof. That no matter what adversity we encounter, his foreknowing of all things causes him to set us in position to be the recipients of his helping hand along our path of life.

It is His pleasure to look for opportunities to bestow blessings on you. Not being predicated on your goodness, but it is based on his goodness that he allows you to receive and gain reflective insight of his grace and mercy. His goodness has a dual purpose. For the saved, it is in the spiritual DNA of God to aggressively run you down and overtake you with goodness and mercy. For the lost, it is a wooing mechanism. I recall before marriage, when I was going out with my, now husband; he could often be found waiting for me in the lobby of my work place with a beautiful bouquet of flowers or a luscious box of chocolates accompanied by a big smile.

The Bible mentions, finding favor in God's sight 133 times. The favor, grace and mercies of God is as a powerful floral bouquet or chocolate delights that are scrumptiously savory to the pallet of one's spirit, designed to draw us close to God, just as I was drawn to my husband by his wooing nature.

Favor, Grace and Mercy in His Sight

Chapter 25

Another Chance

The Social Worker and I returned to the school late that afternoon. Although she attempted to engage me in conversation I elected not to talk much on the way back, but spent that time thinking of how the next 30 days at the school would determine my future. I dosed off several times during the ride as I was beginning to feel a little better. My nerves and my stomach were starting to settle down.

It was almost supper time when I got to my cottage. The girls all wanted to know about my day but I contained my excitement as well as I could and kept much of the information about all that had transpired to myself. I thought somehow if I shared all that took place, this chance to return to regular public high school and live in the same city of my past without living with Aunt Lee would cause this pending opportunity to disintegrate before my very eyes. I was very vague about my interview for the group home and I kept the details to myself, storing it in my heart as a treasure. I took particular care throughout the next 30 days to be on my very best behavior. This opportunity was too important to screw up or be blind-sided by the schemes of the devil. I was particularly careful to avoid possible pitfalls and prayed often that I would encounter no mishaps. My chores were done to perfection as I had always taken pride in doing so. I strived particularly hard to maintain the best grades possible and stayed in my room during most of my free time, just counting the days before I would hear my fate.

Finally, papers came to the cottage announcing my acceptance at the group home along with my departure date. I felt relieved and excited all at the same time. I had been at the school 28 months. I knew growth had taken place within me and I was ready for the next chapter of my life.

Chapter 26

A New Family

As I began packing, I anxiously looked forward to the next move of God in my life with great expectancy. The night before my departure, I tossed and turned throughout the night. Excitement, expectancy, apprehension and hope were building in me all at the same time. Nevertheless, I was ready for what God was going to do next. I had some foresight as to the direction I would be going in but as it is customary; the Lord only reveals so much of our impending future. We are rarely privileged to view the complete picture in advance.

The morning light finally came streaming through the window and I was anxious to rise from my bed for the last time and begin the day. My Social Worker was scheduled to drive me to the city to begin the next phase of my life at noon. I could hardly contain myself through breakfast. I was all packed and ready to go well before time. Finally, I said my goodbyes to everyone. My Social Worker had arrived and she began helping me to load up the belongings that I had accumulated over the past 28 months. We made the trip mostly in silence. I pinched myself several times just to make sure that I was not dreaming and that this was really happening to me.

We didn't go to the group home administrative offices this time, but proceeded straight to the home. We arrived early afternoon and the housemother welcomed me warmly and showed me to my room which I was to share with another girl. I had time to put my things away and come down to the living room area before the girls arrived home from school.

They all went to different schools but I would be going to West Philadelphia High School. There was only one other girl in the house who went to the same school. The girls began trickling in around 3:30 in the afternoon. They were all friendly and each one came into the living room to greet me and introduced themselves as they arrived. My roommate was one of the last ones to arrive as I learned her school was in South Philadelphia and she had a longer ride on public transportation than most of the girls. When she finally arrived, she came straight into the living room and said, "Hi, I'm Helena." I told her my name and immediately Helena and I hit it off.

Helena was a tall slender girl with beautiful caramel colored skin and an equally beautiful smile. The first night we talked almost all night. She wanted to know all about me, and I wanted to know all about her. Helena showed me her long scar which extended down her chest. She had in the past endured open heart surgery. Helena's roots were from South Philadelphia and she shared a great deal about her family that still lived there.

Helena took great care each night to lay out her clothes for the next day as well as her matching costume jewelry. She told me about how things were done at the group home. She, as well as the other girls appeared to be happy and well-adjusted there. They had an excellent cook who came every morning and cooked all of the meals.

After the dinner meal was cooked, she would go home for the day. There were four housemothers that were on the premises in rotating shifts. They each would spend the night during their shift and go home whenever their shift was over.

There was also a housefather that worked evenings on the weekend. He drove us to all of our weekend activities, dances, roller skating, movies etc. He also was responsible for our well-being on such excursions.

Chore day was Saturday. After breakfast, we were responsible to do our assigned chores, which was to clean our rooms and one other house duty. School was in walking distance. On the first day of school I was excited to see how I would measure up and fit in academically. I discovered rather quickly that I was somewhat ahead in my classes and that made me feel really good. There was one girl at school that I remembered from when I lived with Aunt Lee. Her sister Ella, Her and I walked to school together when I was still at Aunt Lee's and now here we were again attending the same school and had the same homeroom teacher and some of the same classes.

One day as we were leaving school for the day, she stopped me and told me that she was glad to see me and had often wondered where I was over the past several years. I thanked her and told her I had gone to a boarding school for a while and was now back living in the city. I didn't bother to go into all the details about how that all came to be. The one thing that she said before we parted that day that has stuck with me over the years was when she said, "You're so quiet and reserved now, you have changed so much. You're not at all like you used to be." I took that as a huge compliment. It was good to know that what had taken place on the inside of me was also outwardly evident.

I walked home that day feeling really good about myself. I was in a good place in my life and I could not have been happier. Computers had just begun to be installed in the High Schools. Once our school got its computer, I recognized it as the same model as I had been trained to use while I was away at boarding school. Our homeroom teacher asked if anyone knew how to operate it. I raised my hand. To my delight, no one else raised their hand. The teacher asked if I would be willing to show him how to operate it. I agreed to do so and within a week's time, he knew the basic functions of that machine. Things were really looking up.

Chapter 27

Settling into the Routine

I was beginning to settle into the day to day routine of the group home. Although we had all come from different backgrounds, we seemed to share a common sisterhood among us and got along fairly well together. During the week, we did our homework after school. (Two days a week we had a tutor that came to help us with our studies.)

Dinner followed and two oblong tables supported all of the girls as well as one housemother. We ate as much as we wanted and afterwards we were given dessert. Whoever had kitchen duty for the week would clear the tables and clean up the kitchen. We had about two hours of free time after dinner. At this time we could make or receive phone calls, watch TV or read. Helena and I would go up to our room and lay out our clothing and matching costume jewelry for the following day.

Helena was boy crazy and was always talking about them. How cute this or that boy was and what he said to her and how he asked for her phone number. (To be honest, 'boy crazy' was a description befitting most of the girls. As a whole, we were going through that stage that girls go through at 15 and 16 years old. During free time, in the back of our minds, we were always waiting for some cute boy whom we had exchanged numbers with, to call. More often than not, the call never materialized. Nevertheless, we had an oath among us that no matter how much we liked a boy, we never called them, they had to call us.

When the expected call did not come, there was a sense of sadness coupled with a strong desire to pick up the phone and dial the young man's number, and although there was a strong desire to relent and make the first move, we all administered strong discouragement to each other against doing so, whenever needed. Our objective was that if the boy really liked you, the call would eventually come (maybe not that night but some future night). We were usually right and when we were wrong, we chalked it up to him not being "the one" anyway. We took great pride in the fact that the oath was never broken, even if it meant going to bed with tears on our faces and disappointment in our hearts.

We were always excited for one another when the phone rang and the housemother would call one of us to the phone. "Kelsey, telephone or Helena, phone." Whoever the lucky girls were that night, we would all be happy for her that her guy called.

The downside was the telephone limitations. We each had 15 minutes and at the end of that time, we had to hang up as there was one phone line and it had to be equally shared among us all. (What we would have done for a cell phone back then).

Saturdays after breakfast and the completion of our chores we each received a small allowance and were permitted free time outside of the house.

We had three hours from 1:00 p.m. until 4:00 p.m. in the afternoon to go to a movie or shop. On more than a few occasions we would take public transportation to another part of town, usually a familiar area or old haunt of one of the girls, in hopes that they would run into an old boyfriend, (probably someone who played a role in them being at the group home in the first place). Sometimes, they would get lucky and see the guy they were looking for and sometimes not. I use the word 'they' as my list of potential boyfriends was practically nonexistent since my immediate past was the all-girls boarding school and my distant past was at Aunt Lee's, neither of which gave me much opportunity to nurture a relationship with the opposite sex. I mostly tagged along to see if something would develop. At any rate, whenever they did see the prospective person they were looking for; they would always pretend that they just happened to be in the area by chance.

The key was to always give the illusion that they were not pursuing but positioning themselves to be pursued. The young man always took the bait and some conversation, a stolen kiss or words of endearment ensued with the promise of a phone call or visit on date night which was on Friday nights from 8:00 p.m. until 11:00 p.m. for girls ages 16 and older. If the young man just happened to have a friend, he would be invited to come along for date night to see if he connected with me or one of the other girls as a prospect for a potential relationship. This was considered a very good and successful three hour free time venture, especially if we were able to accomplish all that we set out to do and still make it back home within the three hour allotted span of time.

Saturday night we went out as a group to a scheduled event. The event was always chaperoned by Mr. Izzy. We all liked Mr. Izzy. He appeared to be in his early 30's and was a graduate of Temple University in Philadelphia. He always seemed to know just the right balance with us girls. Most of the time he had a happy go lucky outward demeanor but he also knew how to put on his serious face when he needed to be firm.

I remember once during Saturday afternoon free time, three of us girls went to a neighborhood where we should not have been and got into a fight. I ended up with a black eye and had to take some of my allowance to buy a pair of sunglasses. At dinner that night, I came to the table with the sunglasses on in an attempt to conceal the black eye.

We stood around the table holding hands as we always did. Mr. Izzy was at the head of the table and he said the grace. We all sat down to eat. Although I tried to avoid eye contact with Mr. Izzy, who was two seats from me and periodically throughout the meal, I could feel his eyes on me. I dreaded the questions that I had conjured up in my mind that he would have been within his rights to ask. Not to mention how embarrassed and foolish I felt sitting in the dining room where there was no sun, with a pair of sun glasses on. I was pleasantly surprised and silently grateful that he never uttered a word regarding the matter.

Chapter 28

Dr. Jekyll

My roommate Helena and I talked about everything. She had recently met a guy named Nick and was totally infatuated with him. We talked about her taking me to meet him as she wanted my opinion of him. Nick and Helena talked on the phone constantly but up to this point, he never came to the home on date night.

One Saturday Helena and I decided we would go to his house on our free time. The problem with that was Nick lived in another town just outside of Philadelphia named, Darby. We would be hard pressed to make it to Darby and back within the limited amount of time we had for free time. But Helena was adamant about going and after much debate about the matter we decided to risk it. We knew there would probably be serious consequences if we were late. (Meaning we would lose our privileges for the next week) but we decided to take the risk.

We had to take the trolley to the end of the line to get there and Nick met us at the last trolley stop as they had previously arranged. We were introduced and Nick, Helena and I walked to his house a few short blocks away. They stood outside talking and I sat on the stoop periodically checking my watch and giving Helena the eye to wrap it up as I did not want to lose my privileges over something I had no stake in. Just as we were about to leave a tall, dark skinned guy with pretty white teeth and a crooked smile came from across the street toward us as he called out "hey Nick what's up man, aren't you going to introduce me to the young lady?"

He nodded his head toward me and Nick said, "This is my girl's best friend, Kelsey." Again he flashed those pearly whites as he extended his hand toward me and introduced himself, "Hi, I'm Jeff." I responded, "Hi, I'm Kelsey." "I know." We both laughed as Jeff sat down next to me on the stoop. We talked for a little while but I kept looking at my watch until Jeff said, "you got someplace to be?" I told him actually we had to get back to the City. Jeff asked if he could see me again and I agreed, inviting him to come to date night in two weeks, (as I was sure Helena and I would not make it back in time to enjoy the privilege of having date night the follow Friday).

The guys walked us to the trolley and waited until we had safely boarded. We waved goodbye to them, as we sat down. We were both in heaven and talked about the guys and what they said during our time together all the way back to the home. Needless to say, we were grounded from the next weekend's activities but we didn't care as we both agreed that the outcome was well worth the punishment.

We finally got our telephone privileges back and the guys called us and made arrangements to come to date night the following weekend. Helena and I could hardly contain ourselves. We planned what we would wear and how we would fix our hair. We often wore one another's clothes and costume jewelry as we were of similar size and height. Friday night finally came and we prepared for the evening ahead. The basement sparkled as we had spent the earlier part of the day cleaning it up and rearranging the sparse furniture.

Kelsey from Pain to Triumph

The mood was set with our favorite music and black light. The guys showed up promptly at 8:00 p.m. Mr. Izzy popped some popcorn for us and brought it to the basement. We had a small frig down there with soft drinks and Kool-Aid. Although Mr. Izzy gave us some space, he would pop down the basement periodically to check on us. I was feeling shy and nervous that night. Jeff was also rather quiet. We didn't talk a lot but we did slow dance. I liked the feel of Jeff's arms around me as we danced. I had very few opportunities in my short lifetime, when I was held close and it was a comforting feeling. For the first time, someone was showing me affection. This was something that I had not experienced since before I went to live with Aunt Lee.

He was soft spoken, complimentary of my appearance and very attentive to me throughout the evening. Our cut off time was 11:00 and Mr. Izzy would flash the light on and off from the top of the stairs, signaling that it was time for company to leave. I didn't want the evening to end but of course it had to. We made plans for Jeff to come again the following Friday and he promised to call me during the week. Jeff had, in my opinion conducted himself like a gentleman throughout the evening. He did not cross my personal boundaries. I welcomed his gentle touch as he held me while we danced, and his soft closed mouth kissed me on the lips goodnight.

After lights out, Helena and I talked into the wee hours of the night. We finally drifted off to sleep just before dawn. I can't remember a time when I felt so good.

Someone cared about me, wanted to get to know me and treated me with loving kindness. I walked around in a fog the next few days. I didn't remember a word the Pastor preached in church that Sunday. My mind was off somewhere in a cloud, thinking about Jeff. When he called that evening, I felt butterflies in the pit of my stomach when I heard his voice. He said he had a good time and looked forward to Friday when we would have date night again. He called every evening and we talked until someone made me give up the phone as I was going beyond my 15 minute limit and other girls needed the use of the phone as well.

Jeff came every Friday to date night and called almost every night during the week. After several months passed, I was head over heels for Jeff and he professed to feel the same. My group counselor who I saw once a month and told her how much I cared for Jeff insisted on meeting him. I was a little hesitant about asking him to come to the City to meet her at the office but I needn't have been. Jeff was cool with it and made himself available for the meeting.

I was 16 at the time and Jeff was 19 going on 20. My counselor thought he was a bit too old for me but I wasn't listening. Jeff also did not have a job and lived at home with his grandmother. None of these things seemed to matter to me. I saw him through rose colored glasses. After all he was always looking for a job but just had not found the right one yet. Now that I think back on that situation, my counselor must have thought that I was dumb as a box of rocks and had no intuitive instinct when it came to Jeff.

After they met and talked alone for a time, she then called me in to join the meeting, I could see that she was not as impressed with him as I was. After Jeff left, she did admit he was very charming, nicely dressed and polite. Outside of that she did not seem to think much of him. Their talk let her know he had no dreams, goals or aspirations in life. I didn't care what she thought, I was in love and nothing could keep us apart. That was one of those situations you think about later in life when you finally have some wisdom and wish your foot could reach your behind, so you could kick yourself in it.

Chapter 29

Marriage Proposal

The following school semester I started my junior year in high school. My school curriculum changed that year to half days in school and half days at work. I was fortunate enough to be selected for a part time clerk position at a local neighborhood finance company. For the first time in my life, I was beginning to feel all grown up. I felt like my life was on track and progressing nicely. Although I was not able to spend my earnings at random, I was given a larger allowance then the girls who did not participate in any type of work study program. I had to open a bank account and each week on pay day I had to deposit all but $20 in my savings account.

My balance began to rise and pretty soon, I had a small nest egg. In my excitement, I told Jeff about my accomplishment. He seemed genuinely happy for me and encouraged me to continue to save my money. Periodically he would casually ask how much I had saved and I would proudly tell him what my current balance had grown to, (I was clueless).

The bank book was stored in the office desk drawer in a lock box and was given to me by the housemother each

Friday so that I could make the current week's deposit from my pay check. Afterward, the bank book was returned to the housemother to store for safe keeping. Life was good! My grades were good at school, my relationship with my house sisters was good, my job was good and Jeff and I were good. I couldn't have been happier. In my mind, this season was most assuredly of mountain top proportions.

Sometimes when the enemy is setting you up, everything appears too good to be true. In my experience, when it looks too good to be true, it more often than not is. One Saturday during free time, I went to Darby alone to meet Jeff's family. For some reason I got the impression that they knew information about Jeff that I was not yet privy to. I can't quite put my finger on what led me to this conclusion. It was basically subtle Innuendos and a feeling in the pit of my belly that sent strong warning signals to my mind. Nevertheless, my mind was not ready to accept what my gut was confirming.

I kept right on thinking that Jeff was the best thing that ever happened to me, so I ignored that feeling in my gut. (I have since learned that the gut does not lie). It confirms dangerous and other negative circumstances that the mind may not be ready to accept. I pushed these thoughts to the back of my mind as I didn't want to spoil the day.

I had to get back to the home as the time was going by rapidly and I didn't want to lose my date night privileges. Jeff walked me to the bus stop and kissed me goodbye with a promise to call to make sure I had made it safely back on time. I made it back with little time to spare. I went to my room and lay across the bed. Helena and the girls were downstairs watching TV. I didn't want to talk about my free time and knew that Helena would ask me what happened. I wasn't ready to talk about meeting Jeff's family or the feeling I had in the pit of my belly. I just lay there thinking about the day's events until I drifted off to sleep.

"Kelsey wake up, the dinner bell rang five minutes ago and we are all waiting for you." I told Helena I would be down in a few minutes. I got up and went to the bathroom to wash my hands and then I went down to the dinner table. Everyone was talking and laughing as we always did at the table. I just ate quickly and asked to be excused. Mr. Izzy said, "Don't you want dessert, we're having peach cobbler and ice cream." I declined and Mr. Izzy looked at me with raised eyebrows, but said okay to my request. Someone said, "What's the matter with her?" I turned and said, "Nothing, I just don't want dessert that's all." I went back to my room and waited for telephone privileges time to start.

A little while later the phone rang and I held my breath expectantly, waiting until I heard Mr. Izzy call up the stairs, "Kelsey" I raced down the stairs smiling and picked up the phone receiver that had been laid on the table.

"Hello." It was Jeff, "Hey baby, did you make it back on time?" "Just barely," I said. We talked awhile and Jeff told me his family liked me and that he would have a surprise for me when he came on Friday. "What is it?" "If I told you, it wouldn't be a surprise, now would it?" I tried to get Jeff to give me a hint, but he would not budge. Some of the girls had started to gather in front of me with their arms folded, scowls on their faces. I knew that was their way of telling me that I was over my time limit and that others needed to use the phone. I told Jeff I had to get off. We said our goodbyes and we both hung up.

Friday finally came and Jeff arrived on time. He had this huge grin on his face as he walked toward me. I was already in the basement putting out the chips and popcorn. None of the other girls had come downstairs yet and Jeff grabbed me and kissed me. I melted as usual and he reached into his pocket and pulled out a small box as he got down on one knee with that big smile on his face. "Kelsey, you know I love you right?" "Yeah, I know." "Well I want you to be my wife. Will you marry me?" My eyes were fixed firmly on the box as he opened it and I held my breath. There nestled in the box was a beautiful engagement ring. "Jeff it's beautiful, where did you get the money?" "Does that mean you will marry me?" "Yes, of course I'll marry you." He pulled me down to him as he held me close and kissed me deeply. My head was spinning as Jeff put the ring on my finger. I forgot all about continuing my line of questioning. Which was, where did he get the money?

We spent the evening whispering and making plans. I didn't tell the girls yet as I wanted to keep it to myself for now. I turned the ring so that the diamond was facing the palm side of my hand as I didn't want anyone to notice the ring and start asking unwanted questions. I did tell Helena as we lay awake talking that night, which we often did after date night. However, I swore her to secrecy and she promised to keep her mouth shut regarding the matter.

I walked around with my head in the clouds for the next few days. I was oblivious to everything around me except Jeff. We planned that I would leave the group home and come to Darby to move in with him and his Grandma until Jeff got a job and we could get our own place. Jeff came to the city that following Monday and we both went to have our blood test done as it was a requirement to get the marriage license. Afterward we had lunch and I went back to the group home that afternoon under the pretense that I had been to school that day. That evening I packed my clothes in my suitcase and Jeff was to meet me after lights out and everyone was asleep. I was nervous as a cat as I packed. Some of the girls came up to the third floor to our room. I decided to tell them all that I was leaving and Jeff and I were engaged to be married. They were all happy for me and the questions began to come from each of them. I answered as best as I could. Not knowing myself exactly what the future held. I only knew that I wanted to be with the one and only man, (outside of my Daddy), who showed me the affection that I so desperately craved and needed.

Chapter 30

Darby Bound

I had managed earlier that evening while the housemother was upstairs to get the key to the lock box in the office where my bank book was stored and get into the box to retrieve my bank book. Later that night after lights were out and the house was quiet, I slipped out of the bed and Helena and I hugged each other and said our goodbyes. I promised to call her as I began to make my way down the stairs as quietly as I could while carrying a suitcase.

I made it to the bottom of the staircase and my heart was beating so fast that I thought it would explode in my chest. I put the suitcase down and tipped over to the window. I could see Jeff across the street pacing back and forth. His coat collar was turned up and his hands were sunk deep in his pockets. I knew he had to be freezing as it was a colder than usual night.

Hurriedly, I got my coat from the closet and quickly unlocked and opened the front door, closing it behind me as I exited the group home for the last time. Jeff saw me and made his way across the street to take my suitcase. He kissed me and said, "I was beginning to think you were not coming." I told him I had to wait until all was quiet in the housemother's room and I knew she was asleep for sure when I heard her snoring as she often did. The girls and I would laugh about it on occasion and say that she *slept like the dead.*

We walked about two blocks until we saw a taxi and Jeff hailed the taxi and told him to take us to Woodland Avenue. We boarded the trolley to Darby 15 minutes later. It was late and we were cold and tired when we got to Darby. Jeff had the suitcase in one hand and my other hand and his occupied his pocket as we made our way up the block to Jeff's house. His Grandma was still up watching TV when we arrived and told us that she had made the bed in the spare bedroom for me to sleep in. Jeff tried to convince her that we should both sleep in his room but she would not budge on that issue. "You all are not married yet." I didn't put up a fuss. Though I loved Jeff deeply, I was secretly grateful as I had some apprehensions about sleeping with him, and I realized at that point that I had not thought that part of it through. I was exhausted and slept soundly that night.

I woke the following morning to find the sun streaming in the window over my face and Jeff standing over me with that charismatic smile on his face. "Good morning," I whispered good morning back to him as I asked, "what time is it?" Jeff said it was almost 10:00 a.m. I got out of the bed and went to the bathroom to relieve my full bladder. I had an anxious feeling in the pit of my stomach as I thought to myself that the housemother at the group home must be frantic with worry as I didn't leave her a note or anything, and I knew the girls would not disclose my whereabouts to her.

Here it was a school day and a work day and I was no longer in position to participate in school or work. I hadn't thought about how this move would affect my life. For the first time, I started to realize that I was underage and the housemother would have to notify the police that I was missing and that would limit my mobility to work. I didn't want to involve Jeff or his Grandma as I was now officially considered a runaway.

I asked Jeff where his Grandma was and he said, "She left this morning to take care of some business." I hoped that "business" didn't include going to the police about me. I was jumpy and everyone was a suspect in my mind regarding my whereabouts. I asked Jeff if he thought she would say anything to the police about me being there and he looked at me rather funny and said, "Who Nana? No silly, of course not."

I was sitting on the edge of the bed with my pajamas still on as Jeff walked over and stood between my legs grabbing both of my hands and playfully pinning me down on the bed for a kiss. My body tensed and Jeff looked at me. "Don't," I whispered. He saw the fear on my face and he let go of my hands and quietly turned and said, "I'm going to make us breakfast," "Okay, I'll jump in the shower while you're doing that."

I took a long shower and got dressed in the bathroom. I was beginning to realize that perhaps I wasn't as grown up as I thought I was. Jeff was 20 and I hadn't even had my 17th birthday yet. For the first time, I began to wonder if I had moved too quickly. I loved Jeff but I wasn't ready to go all the way yet. What was I thinking? I suddenly wanted to go back to the group home. I wanted things to be back the way they were before Jeff proposed. I felt safe and secure then. Now I was a jittery, anxious hot mess.

After a breakfast of eggs, bacon and toast, (which I hardly touched), Jeff asked me if everything was alright. I told him about my thoughts and fears and he held me and told me not to worry.

He assured me that he wouldn't rush me to make love and he said that he wanted us to go to New York after we were married. Darby was too close to the city and he didn't want me to feel afraid that the police would come after me. I agreed. My insides began to settle down a little and we enjoyed the rest of the day, just being together.

Chapter 31

Mr. Hyde

Jeff's grandmother came in late in the afternoon. She had to walk up a flight of stairs and she pulled a shopping cart behind her. She was sweating when she walked in the door and immediately took off her coat and sat down in the living room. Jeff said, "Nana what's wrong?" "I'm just feeling a little faint," she said. (I wondered why Jeff didn't mention to her that she should have called upstairs for him to come down to help her or put the groceries away for her). "Miss Liz, can I put the groceries away for you?" "Would you please?" "Sure," I said.

Jeff on the other hand, sat down by his grandmother. He told her that we wanted to get a license to get married but I was only 16. (You had to be 18 to sign for yourself). He had hatched some hair brained scheme in his head for her to go with us and say she was my guardian and that my parents were both dead and had left me in her care, that way she could sign for me to marry Jeff. (Personally, I didn't think she had it in her to do. She just didn't seem like the type to be able to tell a believable lie). "I don't know Jeffrey," she said. "I don't feel good about this. Why don't you all just wait until next year when Kelsey turns 18?" Jeff became angry and began yelling at his grandmother that he didn't see the big deal and how she never wanted to do anything for him. She was visibly upset and after his outburst, she relented and agreed to help us. Something inside of me started to feel anxious and jittery again. I wondered why Jeff was in such a hurry and what was wrong with waiting like his grandmother suggested?

My throat was dry and for some reason, I was afraid to tell him that I didn't mind waiting. I had never heard Jeff raise his voice before. Nor had I seen anger on his face like I had that day.

The following day we all showered, dressed and prepared to go downtown to City Hall to get the license. Jeff didn't have the money for the license and asked me to pay for it out of my savings. I didn't want to experience his wrath so I agreed. He grilled his grandmother all the way to the City, telling her what to say if they asked this question or that question. I could tell she was flustered and this would be a very difficult thing for her to pull off. Jeff seemed oblivious to what she was going through and continued his badgering until we arrived at City Hall.

I was nervous as a cat. My head was spinning but I managed to appear outwardly calm. A tall stately lady looked up from behind the counter and called, "next" and the three of us went up to the counter. Jeff spoke first and said, "We're here to apply for a marriage license." She handed Jeff a form and told us to fill it out and give it back to her when it was completed. We sat down and Jeff pushed the form in my hand and told me to fill it out. I answered the questions the best that I could. We waited for what seemed like an eternity after Jeff gave the completed form back to the clerk.

Finally the clerk called us up and led us to a cubicle. She began to ask some of the questions that Jeff had grilled his grandmother to answer. She separated me and Jeff from

Kelsey from Pain to Triumph

his grandmother, questioning us about how I came to live with them and how long I had been in his grandmother's care.

Jeff said I had lived with her about two years. The clerk called Jeff's grandmother back into the cubicle with us and the first question she asked was how long had I been in her care. Jeff's grandmother looked up at the ceiling and she said, "Oh about six years or so." That was it, our story had fallen apart.

The clerk took the money for the license but we were to bring back the documents the next day to show that Jeff's grandmother had been appointed legal guardian over me and the license would be given to us at that time.

I cried all the way back to Darby. Jeff was scowling and sputtering profanities, telling his grandmother that it was her fault that the plan didn't work. She just kept saying she was sorry, and that she had done the best she could. I couldn't believe my ears. This was a side of Jeff I did not know. I was shaken by the whole situation to include abruptly leaving the group home, the disconnect from school and work, uprooting myself from the girls I had begun to think of as family, Jeff's behavior and the whole lie that was concocted and told to the Clerk at City Hall. I was also annoyed that I spent my money for a license that we were obviously not going to get as Jeff's brilliant plan had backfired.

Jeff was moody for the next couple of days. But by the third day, plan "B" had started to take shape in his mind. Jeff had come into my room that next morning and by the time I woke up he was sitting at the edge of the bed with a big grin on his face.

"Good Morning," he said. I said good morning to him. "Kelsey, I've been thinking." "About what," I said. "Let's blow this town baby. There *ain't* no future for us here. How about I go to New York, look for a job and get us set up. You can stay here with Nana and work. You know, save a little money on this end while I get things straight on the other end for us. Then I can send for you and we can start our life together."

"Jeff, I really don't want to be separated from you and I sure as heck don't want to be a burden to your grandmother." "It won't be long baby, just until we can see our way clear," he said. Even though I didn't like the idea of living with Jeff's grandmother while he went to New York, I agreed to go along with Jeff's plan as I wasn't keen on us living off her when we were young and well able to work. Especially since my savings had dwindling down to nothing. I was giving Jeff's grandmother money to help out with groceries. She was on a fixed income and I felt some kind of way about her spending her small income to feed us, not to mention how much it must have increased her electric bill with Jeff sitting up watching TV half the night.

Although I didn't eat that much, Jeff's appetite was ferocious. He would eat six slices of bacon and four to five eggs for breakfast every day. His grandmother started to limit him to four strips of bacon and three eggs a day for breakfast. She often used pancakes or French toast as a filler to satisfy his huge appetite. Jeff refused to eat cereal yet his contribution was "0" and he made no effort to look for work in Darby.

I started to look in the paper on Sundays and found work through a temp agency doing housework for private homes. I would get up at 5:00 a.m. in the morning, shower and dress and be out the door to go catch the bus by 6:00 a.m. I often traveled an hour or more to and from work. The home owners I worked for were well to do and they took advantage of my youth, working me extremely hard for the eight hour shift from the moment I arrived until the moment I left while paying me the minimum allowable wage. The only good part about the job was that I got paid daily. As soon as I had saved Jeff's so called "startup" cost, he took the money; packed a small suitcase and insisted on leaving in the middle of the night to catch a bus to New York. After Jeff left, I continued working and I came back to Darby every night so exhausted I often showered and went straight to bed after dinner. Each night I thought just before sleep overtook me, this was not the life I had envisioned for myself.

Time did nothing to change the negative feeling that kept gnawing at my gut. It was a feeling that enforced the notion that I had made a mistake but my heart continued to ignore my gut. Not to mention that I couldn't just pack up and waltz back to the City and back into the group home environment as if nothing had happened. During a rare but brief telephone conversation with Helena, I found out that one of the girls had ratted me out to the group home housemother. I felt I was at the point of no return and I would have to gather my courage and forge ahead believing the best in spite of what my gut feeling was telling me.

Jeff called almost every night to ask me how work was going and to see if I was still working. He would also update me on the progress on his end. Just hearing his voice when he would say, "Kelsey, you know I love you girl. I can't wait until we are together again." Jeff was very charming and he knew just what to say to get my heart racing. His constant reference to his "love" for me was something that I was not accustomed to hearing in my past and it was like a drug to my very soul.

The following night when Jeff called he was excited, he had found a place for us to live and wanted me to pack up and head to New York right away. Although he had not found a job yet, he assured me that he was looking diligently and he felt sure something was about to change for the better in that area. I packed my suitcase that night preparing to leave the following morning. I had that nervous feeling in my gut again as I tossed and turned all night. I was extremely restless. Uncertainty had a way of clutching at my emotions to the point of uneasiness but as always, I pushed those feelings deep into the lower recesses of my mind, ignoring every sign as if it were a delusion.

Daylight finally found its way into the room and as soon as it appeared I got up and showered, dressed and put the last few things in my suitcase. Jeff's grandmother must have heard me stirring around. Even though I tried my best not to wake her, she was knocking at the door. "Come in," I said and she opened the door. "Good Morning, Kelsey." "Good morning'" I said. "I was about to start breakfast, are you hungry?" "No Ma'am." My stomach was in knots and I knew I wouldn't be able to eat a thing.

"Well, let me make you some sandwiches in case you get hungry on the bus ride." Jeff's grandmother was very sweet and always giving and offering to give what little she had. "No, really I'm good. Please don't go to any trouble I couldn't eat a thing." "You sure, it's no trouble at all?" "Yes Ma'am, I'm sure." "Okay," she said reluctantly.

I made the bed for the last time and a few minutes later I was at the door, suitcase in hand, hugging her and thanking her for all she had done for me. She had opened her home to me and went out of her way to make me feel at home. Sometimes I would sit in the kitchen and watch her cook. She taught me how to make sweet potato pie and though I never wrote down the recipe, I can visualize each step of the process that she guided me through and I can almost hear her soft voice lovingly giving me instructions each time I have made it throughout the years. She hugged me tight and told me to have a safe trip and to let her know when I had arrived safely.

Kelsey from Pain to Triumph

I walked the short distance to the bus terminal. The suitcase was heavy but I managed to carry it, switching hands along the way. I had saved a little nest egg again as I had only purchased necessities and given Jeff's grandmother money weekly to help out. Even though she never wanted to take it, I would insist as I didn't want to be a financial burden to her.

I bought my ticket to New York and soon afterward, I was standing in front of the bus as the driver took my suitcase and put it in the luggage compartment of the bus. I waited for him to close the compartment and take my ticket before stepping up onto the bus.

Minutes later, the bus pulled out and we were on our way. To my surprise I slept all the way and was astonished when we arrived in New York. I thought it would take much longer to get there but it was less than a two hour trip. My nerves were still on edge as I exited the bus and waited for my suitcase. I called Jeff at the motel where he had been staying and he came to pick me up within 15 minutes.

I looked up and there he was walking toward me with that charming swagger and brilliant smile. Our eyes locked, he reached his arms out to me and pulled me close, "I missed you girl," he said. "I missed you too." Jeff grabbed my suitcase with one hand and put his other arm around me. We began to walk toward the motel where Jeff had been staying. I was disappointed when we arrived. The motel was a bit run down and the clientele congregating in front of the place looked very seedy to say the least. Jeff walked me straight to the front desk clerk and introduced me as his wife. I nodded my head in greeting and Jeff whispered to me that he was a little behind in paying and asked me to pay the clerk the $70 that he was past due and also the weekly rate for the upcoming week.

I reluctantly paid the clerk as I wondered what the heck Jeff had been doing these past few months. He told me numerous times that he was doing odd jobs and day labor to stay afloat until something better came along. I could see that nothing better had come along and we were no further ahead at this point then we were when he left Darby.

I wasn't ready to start an argument with him about his progress or the lack thereof but I was beginning to feel like Jeff was taking advantage of me.

My worst fears were confirmed when he took me to a nearby temp agency the next day and they found work for me right away. I started doing day labor as a housekeeper and was paid daily. Each day after work I would come back to the motel and put most of the money in a little pouch in the drawer. I was saving for the studio apartment Jeff had talked about, so that we could move. I hated the motel where we stayed and couldn't wait to get out of there.

Jeff pretended to look for work but claimed he couldn't find anything steady. One day after I had been there for about a month, I came back to the motel from work. I took the money I earned from my wallet and opened the little pouch I had been saving money in from the dresser drawer, to my surprise, the pouch was empty.

Jeff came in moments after with a new outfit on and a new pair of shoes. I could smell the stench of alcohol on his breath. I was furious.

"Where is the money Jeff?"

"Baby, I'm going to pay you back just as soon as I start working. Nobody's *gonna* hire me looking like a bum. I needed some new clothes."

Jeff and I had our first fight that day. I was livid with rage and I pushed Jeff and began screaming at him and calling him names that I cannot repeat. Jeff grabbed me and slapped me hard across the face. I sunk down on the bed and began to cry. Jeff had never hit me before and I was beginning to feel like my situation was hopeless.

I didn't eat dinner that night and I slept in my clothes with my day's wages in my bra. I woke up early the following morning but I didn't get out of the bed. I was uncomfortable from sleeping in my clothing. My face was sore, (reminding me of what had transpired the night before). I lie there trying to think of a plan that would deter Jeff from taking money from me in the future. The motel room was so small, I could not think of a hiding place where he would not be likely to find it.

I was sick with grief regarding the turn of events. This was not the fairy tale life I had envisioned. I was beginning to see a side of Jeff that I didn't like. He was lazy and reckless with money. Taking what he had not earned and throwing it away frivolously. He had little regard or ambition for a better life. How did I get myself into this mess?

One minute I'm on track, living in the group home with structure, guidance and a sisterhood that I valued. Going to school and getting good grades and working part time and earning my own money, only to find myself in a situation where I felt hopeless and helpless.

Jeff and I had become intimate once I got to New York but even that aspect of the relationship was not what I expected it to be. I was disappointed as I had imagined that two people experiencing something as beautiful as the intimacy and bonding that I expected to occur during such a special time would be greater than no other. However, each time that we came together, I was left feeling unfulfilled and thought to myself, "is that all there is?"

I thought perhaps something was wrong with me that I was not able to take pleasure in our coming together. As time went on I began to make excuses in order to avoid being intimate with him. This did not go over well with Jeff and he would often show his displeasure with bad behavior.

Jeff began drinking more and more. I dreaded those times as I knew the outcome of his drinking was to my detriment. Once after drinking a bottle of wine and sulking over the previous night's rejection, he ordered me to dance for him. I was tired from working and in no mood to honor his request. I refused. Jeff became very angry and grabbed me in my collar and proceeded to rip my blouse down the front.

The buttons from my shirt popped off and landed all over the floor. I begged him to stop but he continued to pull and rip the clothing from my body. I was helpless to stop him. Jeff had his way with me that night. I cried myself to sleep. Mr. Hyde was showing up more and more every day. I prayed consistently each day. Even the position of my hands clasped together, on my knees in silent prayer made him angry. He would say, "I know you praying to be rid of me, you better pray!" And pray, I did. As I look back, I remember the prayer being one that I have heard many women pray throughout my years. It was that age old prayer that says, "Lord if you just get me out of this situation, I promise never to get involved with a man like this again." Sound familiar?

The work as housekeeper was also beginning to take an emotional toll on me. The family I cleaned house for had two children. The younger one was about four years old and I was tasked to wipe her behind after each bathroom visit. She would call to me no matter where I was in the home or what I was doing and say. "Kelsey, I need you to wipe my butt." I began the process of not only cleaning her private parts but also teaching her how to clean herself. She seemed reluctant to learn as she had not been taught that this was a task that she would one day be expected to do for herself.

One day I overheard her tell a playmate that I was "her maid" and if she had to use the restroom, that I would clean her afterwards. This was troubling to me as I didn't perceive it to be part of my daily duties to clean her or her playmates behind. I decided one day that I would let the agency know that I wished to seek employment in a different career field. They gave me forms to fill out to identify my skills and encouraged me to come every day after work to enhance my typing speed. I was permitted to use their typewriter and I would go there straight from work each day for one hour and practice my typing speed. When my speed had increased sufficiently, I was given a standard achievement test and scored high enough for the agency to begin sending me to other jobs more suitable to my potential. I never returned to cleaning houses for a living again.

I was often told I was slow when I first arrived in the Big Apple and that was considered a liability in such a fast paced city. I made it my priority to learn to work and move more quickly and efficiently.

This trait was the key that unlocked the door to a permanent clerical position. Once I had achieved this skill, so to speak, I was able to earn more money.

Jeff finally landed a job as a security guard and we were able to move into a small furnished apartment in the Bronx. Things seemed to be looking up as Jeff didn't have so much time on his hands and therefore did not drink as much. Work minus alcohol meant that I would experience more of Dr. Jekyll and less of Mr. Hyde.

We still struggled more than we should have but neither of us had lived on our own and paid rent, utilities as well as food and clothing. Our limited experience in managing money caused us to make poor decisions. Often we had to buy groceries on credit at the neighborhood corner grocery store. This meant that at the end of each week as we got paid we took turns paying the large grocery bill we had accumulated buying food on credit throughout the week. The large grocery store would have been less expensive but it was not nearby and we had not factored that in when we rented the apartment. Jeff's appetite was ferocious and if he bought four pork chops on credit he wanted to eat three of them. On one occasion, I was particularly hungry as I had not eaten lunch that day. I cooked the chops Jeff brought home from the store. That night I wanted two chops but Jeff would not hear of it. He slapped me when I would not agree to let him eat three chops and I eat only one. I was so angry at his selfishness that I went to bed that night without eating at all.

Conclusion

    I woke up feeling sick the next morning. I ate a bowl of cereal thinking that my stomach was upset because I had not eaten since breakfast the morning before. Shortly after I ate the cereal, the room began to spin and I barely made it to the bathroom before throwing up. I didn't feel well the next couple of days and started to think back in my mind when I last had my monthly cycle. I calculated that I was overdue a couple of weeks.

    I didn't say anything to Jeff as I thought perhaps I had missed a cycle due to the emotional distress of bills, work and the anxiety of not knowing when Jeff was going to turn into Mr. Hyde again. Another month went by and I didn't get my cycle again. Certain smells throughout the day would trigger an episode of violent sickness. I knew I had to go to the doctor.

    A coworker told me about a free clinic near the job. I decided to go during my lunch break. The nurse at the front desk of the clinic greeted me with a smile. She gave me some forms on a clip board to fill out and sign. Shortly after filling out the forms my name was called and I was given a tube with instructions and told to go into the bathroom and use the tube to collect a urine sample. Afterward, the nurse said they would call me within a day or two to give me the results.

I spent that night tossing and turning. Sleep finally came about two hours before my normal time to get up. Jeff always left the apartment before me as he had a longer distance to travel to work then I did. I woke up late that morning and started rushing to get ready. Just as I was about to leave the apartment to catch the bus, the phone rang. I rushed to pick up the telephone. It was the nurse at the clinic calling to say my urinalysis had come back positive. I was pregnant.

I had mixed emotions about this new status of my life. Part of me was happy that there would be another person in my life that I could shower my love on that would love me back unconditionally. Part of me had some doubts as Jeff and I were not in a good place. Nevertheless, I hoped that this child would be instrumental in creating change for the better in our relationship. I decided to wait until later that evening after work to tell Jeff the news. I wanted a time to just bask in that moment by myself.

On the way home that evening, I stopped at the grocer and got a chuck steak. I didn't want to buy the steak on store credit and I didn't have much money to splurge so the desired T-bone was out of the question. I was not doing half bad with cooking. I had a good recipe that I had been anxious to try. It was fairly easy to prepare and by the time Jeff got home it was almost ready. The steak turned out good and I added baked potatoes and a salad to the meal.

Jeff ate heartily, (as was his custom). He genuinely seemed to enjoy the meal. I was glad he was in a good mood and even offered to help with the dishes. Once in awhile the old Jeff that I fell in love with would emerge and I was grateful that tonight was one of those times. It was the perfect scenario for my news.

After, I finished the dishes I went into the living room where Jeff was lounging in front of the TV. I sat down beside him and he looked at me with raised eyebrows, seemingly surprised that I didn't head to the bedroom, as I had avoided being in his presence lately. (I never knew when something I said or did would trigger an unwanted reaction from him. So in order to keep the peace I had begun steering clear of Jeff as much as possible). But tonight I would risk it. "Jeff," "Hmmm," he said half listening, with his attention more on the television program. "You know I haven't been feeling well lately." "Yeah I know." "Well, I went to a clinic near work yesterday." "I was given a urine test. The nurse at the clinic called me today with the results." Jeff looked over at me at that moment. "We are going to have a baby."

A big smile, spread across his face and he drew me close. "Honey, are you sure?" "Yes, I'm sure." "Oh honey, that's great." He laid his hand on my belly. "Let's call Nana and tell her." Jeff seemed genuinely happy about the news and I could see the excitement in his eyes as he shared the news with his grandmother. This was the Jeff that I had fallen in love with. Perhaps this baby was just what we needed to turn things around. I went to sleep that night, hopeful that things would change for the better.

For the most part, Jeff showed a very loving and caring side of himself that I rarely saw prior to the pregnancy. His security guard job was at a retail shop that sold a line of maternity clothes among other things. His boss offered to give him a sizable discount for the maternity wear and Jeff took me there to try on and purchase the clothing.

He knew that we were a struggling young couple and offered to allow Jeff to pay for the merchandise by having payments deducted from his wages each pay period until the balance was paid in full and he accepted the offer.

During the pregnancy, I felt compelled to reach out to Aunt Lee and Uncle J.T. I thought it was time that they knew that I was okay and to catch them up on what had transpired since I left the group home. After all, they were family and I wanted them to know that I was okay (I didn't mention anything about Jeff's abusive behavior toward me). Aunt Lee was happy to hear from me and to know that I was alive and well. I told her about the baby, also. She wasn't too happy about that part and tried to convince me to give the baby up for adoption when it was born. I was disappointed at her suggestion and I refused, telling her that I wanted my baby and I wasn't going to give it up. After much conversation about the matter, she reluctantly gave up trying to convince me to give the baby up at birth.

Aunt Lee reminded me that we had family members that lived in New York and encouraged me to contact them. She gave me the telephone numbers of two other aunts, (younger sisters of hers), that lived in the same city with me. This was good news. It was comforting to know that I had family nearby.

She also called them and gave them my telephone number. Shortly afterward they came for a visit along with my younger cousins. I had not seen these family members in many years but once we were together, it was as though we had never been separated. We had a great time during their visit. They got in the kitchen and cooked and we ate and laughed and reminisced about old times.

All was going well until Jeff and one of my cousins disappeared. After looking all over the apartment, it was discovered that they were both locked in the small second bedroom in the back of the apartment.

After five minutes of my aunt Dee Dee banging on the back bedroom door and telling them to open the door, they finally unlocked the door and emerged both of them looking unkempt and sheepish with some lame excuse about why they had disappeared in that bedroom and had the door locked.

My family took a strong dislike toward Jeff after that incident. I was mortified and could not understand why Jeff would do such a thing the very first time that he met members of my family. They left shortly afterwards, and Jeff and I had a big fight that evening. The fight resulted in him spitting in my face, (not once, but twice). I just sank to the floor crying hysterically not able to comprehend how I had gotten myself in such a fix. Things couldn't be worse. I slept in the spare bedroom that night and had very little to say to Jeff during the rest of that week. He walked around acting and talking like I had done something wrong to him, stating that I had embarrassed him and I was being insecure for no reason.

I kept my mouth shut as I tried to swallow the lump that appeared in my throat continually while I fought back bitter tears in silence. My love for him turned to hatred. I was appalled at his ability to twist things to make it seem like I was the culprit and he had done nothing wrong. The spitting in the face was played over and over in my mind and each time I replayed the scene back in my head, made me dislike him all the more.

I warded off Jeff's advances and attempts to apologize and make things right. I just couldn't get pass what happened. Jeff started to drink a lot again and that meant bad news for me as I would be the subject of his Mr. Hyde personality.

My belly was getting big and my feet were swollen. In my eighth month of pregnancy, I was let go from my job. I was miserable and worried about the financial aspect due to there being only one income now. Jeff started going out on Friday nights. I was actually grateful for those times of peace and solitude. I would spend much of that time in prayer talking to God as I often did, asking him what I should do about my bleak situation. Many times, Jeff wouldn't come home until the next morning. He would stumble in drunk, demanding that I get up and fix him something to eat. Often times he would be dead sleep by the time the food was prepared and it would sit there until it was no longer edible and had to be thrown in the trash.

Not only had my love faded for Jeff, I didn't even like him anymore. How in the world did I get myself into this mess? I was so sure that Jeff was the man for me. Now I could hardly stand the sight of him. He was so different from the man I fell in love with. I prayed often that God would show me a way out.

One Saturday morning in early November, while making breakfast I felt something wet running down my leg. I ran to the bathroom to see what was happening. Water was running down my leg continuously and I realized that my water had broken.

After telling Jeff, he called his grandmother and although it was a month before my due date, she told him that he needed to get me to the hospital. We called first and told them my symptoms and they suggested that we come in. We took a taxi to the hospital and after a doctor examined me, I was admitted and given a room with three other ladies. My membrane had ruptured and the doctor wanted to watch me. Nothing happened that day and I slept most of the day. Jeff went back home late that evening. The following day after lunch, I began to feel nauseated. I threw up and the doctor was called. He examined me and said that I was dilating and I was going to be transferred to the labor room. I was given two shots, (one in each thigh). The doctor left me alone and although I felt contractions, I was still able to go to sleep. Several hours later the door was opened and the light was turned on. The doctor said it was time for me to push as my baby was ready to come. Two pushes later, my beautiful baby girl was born.

The nurse took her and cleaned her up and then she was whisked away to be placed in an incubator. She weighed four pounds and 11 ounces and was so beautiful and tiny. Later I was taken back to the room that I was put in originally when I was admitted. Later that day I tried to go to the baby room to see my beautiful baby girl again but I felt faint and had to turn around and go back to the room after only walking part of the way to her incubation room.

Jeff was in the room sitting beside my bed when I returned. He informed me that her name would be Dorian. I was not asked what I thought about the name or if I had a preference regarding the name.

It would be Dorian and that was that. I have no idea how he came up with the name and I really didn't care. Nothing could spoil my mood, I had a beautiful tiny little baby girl. I didn't want to spoil it arguing with Jeff about a name. A few days later, I was wheeled to the hospital entrance and Jeff took me home. We both felt a little sad that we weren't able to bring the baby home with us. The doctor said that she needed to be at least five pounds.

Jeff had to work but I went to the hospital every day to feed the baby and check on her progress. She was gaining weight but not as fast as we would have liked. When Dorian finally weighed five pounds, the doctor suggested that she stay in the hospital until she weighed a few more ounces. He explained that babies often lose weight once they go home before they start to gain. Jeff wasn't having it. He took off from work and stated we were going to get Dorian and he didn't care what the doctor said. As much as I wanted her home, I was a little afraid that maybe we should leave her in the hospital until the doctor was ready to release her. Jeff was adamant about her coming home now. His mind was made up and I didn't want to get into a fight with him about it.

Once at the hospital, he made me do all the talking. The doctor finally relented against his better judgment but made me sign a statement that said he would not be held liable if something happened to Dorian. That settled it and we took Dorian home that day. We didn't have the money for a crib, so I emptied a dresser drawer and cleaned it out. I lined it with a sheet and added a soft pillow with a freshly washed pillow case on it.

The drawer was placed between two kitchen chairs facing each other and set up by my side of the bed. Dorian slept most of the time and I had to wake her every three to four hours to feed and change her. I hardly slept at night as I kept jumping up looking at her and holding a small compact mirror to her little nose to make sure she was still breathing. Jeff slept like a baby and offered no help.

Financially, we were struggling as Dorian's need for formula, clothing, diapers, special laundry detergent, etc. exceeded the budget. At the first well baby clinic appointment I was given information about temporary benefits for babies who were born premature. I filled out the paperwork and mailed it the same day, praying, as always for God's intercession and guidance on how to hold everything together. The telephone had been disconnected as we could no longer afford to keep it on.

Several weeks passed before I received a letter in the mail telling me that I had been given an appointment to come in and bring certain documents in order to complete the process for temporary assistance. I was grateful that the office address was close enough that I could walk to it, but it was winter and I didn't want to chance Dorian getting sick. I was able to arrange for my aunt Dee Dee to come over and watch her while I went to the appointment.

Kelsey from Pain to Triumph

Except for the waiting time, everything went smoothly and when I left I had an emergency check in hand. I was relieved and so thankful, to say the least that God had made a way of provision, even though I was becoming more acutely aware that I had not done things in a manner that warranted the blessings that I had received. I prayed within myself for forgiveness.

Although Jeff continued to work and was fairly quiet in the evenings when he got home, things were strained between us and I found myself giving all of my attention to Dorian. On Friday nights Jeff came home with several bottles of wine in hand. I knew that meant Mr. Hyde would be rearing his ugly head and there was no telling how bad things would get.

I always prayed that he would pass out from drinking before his wrath would come down on me. The times that he didn't pass out, I was subject to his verbal and physical attacks.

Since Dorian was born she was the center of my world, and I had become pretty much numb to all of Jeff's shenanigans and he didn't like it one bit. He was always angry that I had basically shut him out emotionally and sexually. When he got fed up with it, he would beat me and call me all kinds of dirty names before taking what he wanted from me. He didn't seem to be satisfied unless he was able to reduce me to tears. Once satisfied that he had gotten the reaction he so craved, he would then drift off to sleep in a drunken stupor.

Aunt Dee Dee would come by during the day and help out with washing the baby's diapers. She often brought a cute little outfit for Dorian. I hid the gory details of my relationship with Jeff from her although she could see that I was not happy with him and asked me constantly if everything was alright.

"You know you don't have to put up with no stuff from him, you and the baby can come and stay with me." I assured her that everything was okay, (even though she could tell that it wasn't).

She made it clear that she didn't like Jeff as she was able to discern some things about him that did not put him in a very favorable light. I didn't want her to worry and I didn't want her to do anything to Jeff that would get her into trouble. Aunt Dee Dee was very family oriented and protective. She had a reputation for always keeping a batch of lye brewed up for those who tried to bring harm to her or any family member. I have been told that she would not hesitate to use it if she felt the situation called for it.

One Friday night after Jeff got drunk he came into the bedroom where I was. Dorian was sound asleep and I was reading as I often did to pass the time. He had that angry look on his face as was so often apparent these days. He walked swiftly toward me without a word and before I knew it, he was snatching the book from my hands, throwing it to the floor. "Jeff, please not tonight. "Jeff please my a_ _," he retorted. Not again, I thought as I put my hands to my head. "Maybe this will get your attention," he said. He snatched Dorian out of the drawer where she was sleeping peacefully and began to toss her up in the air, almost touching the ceiling. Dorian's little body jumped and a blood curdling scream escaped her lips. "Jeff, please stop it." I reached for Dorian but Jeff knocked me to the floor as he reached out to catch her as she came down and threw her high in the air again catching her as she came down a second time.

Dorian and I both were crying hysterically as I begged him to stop. "Oh I got your attention now?" He shoved Dorian into my arms and said, "Shut her up before I throw her on the floor and kill her." At that moment, I hated Jeff and knew that I had to do something to get away from him.

I didn't know what, I just knew that somehow with God's help, I would have to make a change and soon.

Once Jeff left the room, I held Dorian and rocked her in my arms as the tears ran down my cheeks. She finally stopped crying and drifted back to sleep. Soon after, I could hear Jeff snoring in the living room. I found myself crying out to God again for relief. How I could have been so wrong about Jeff was beyond my comprehension. His former charm, and whispers of his love for me, totally swept me off my feet. I had given up everything to be with him. Dorian was the only good thing to come out of our relationship. I would do anything to take it all back with the exception of her. She was the reason I was able to go on each day.

As usual after a Mr. Hyde episode, Jeff was quite the day after. He would walk around with an apologetic look on his face. Looking at him now I couldn't believe that just the previous night he had been so hurtful to Dorian. These latest shenanigans turned my heart cold as ice toward him. I knew I was unyielding in my emotions but I couldn't shake the mental picture that was stamped in my mind from the night before. It was one thing to treat me badly but doing it to Dorian was another thing. I vowed that somehow I would get away from him.

It was Saturday morning, Jeff went downstairs to get the mail and my temporary assistance check had come. He showered and dressed without a word. Afterward, he handed me the check to sign and mumbled that he was going to the store to pick up a few things and asked me did I need anything. I said no, not even looking at him.

Shortly afterward, Jeff came back with a bag from the store. He brought it into the kitchen and set it on the table. For a change he didn't demand that I fix him breakfast but started to put the contents of the bag on the table. He had bought a dozen eggs, a package of bacon, a loaf of bread and some orange juice. I was standing at the sink washing diapers as he stated he was going out and would be back later. He left me no money from my own check, (which was also his custom). I didn't dare ask as I couldn't risk another scene right now.

The day went by peacefully. I made breakfast for myself and after eating I bathed and dressed Dorian. She was a bit jumpy all day and my heart went out to her. Neither of us deserved the kind of treatment that we were getting. Even though Jeff would often make threats that if I ever left him, he would find me and kill me.

For Dorian's sake, I had to risk it as my fear was greater for her safety then my own. I knew I had to find a job and a good daycare for Dorian so that I could get my baby away from him. Jeff didn't come home that night or the next day. By Monday afternoon, Dorian was down to her last can of milk and still no sign of Jeff.

How could he go off like that and leave us with no money while he was gallivanting around, (who knows where). I bathed and dressed the baby and myself and took her out to the grocery store to get her some milk. The owner stated that Jeff hadn't paid the bill in two weeks and that he could no longer extend us credit. I was embarrassed and angry as I walked out of the store. I took Dorian back upstairs and started packing her diaper bag with her essentials and an overnight bag for myself. As much as I hated to do it, I would have to put Dorian in the stroller and walk the four mile distance to my Aunt Dee Dee's house as I didn't even have bus fare. Things could not be worse.

Even though it was December, I was grateful that it wasn't too cold that day. I bundled Dorian up good and started out on the long walk. When I arrived, Aunt Dee Dee didn't look surprised to see me. She said, "I was going to take a cab over to your apartment today as soon as I got finished cleaning up. Your so called husband, done got his self in trouble and is in jail." Our telephone was disconnected as Jeff hadn't paid the bill. It seems he called Aunt Dee Dee collect asking her to bail him out. She told him that she didn't have the money to bail him out. (She never liked Jeff and often told me that he gave her the creeps whenever he looked at her). "Collect?" I said dumbfounded. "Yeah, I made some calls and found out he was arrested Saturday night for drunk and disorderly conduct in some bar in downtown Philly."

    I finally got to talk to the desk sergeant at the precinct and he told me normally they lock them up until they sleep it off and release them the following day on their own recognizance. But, the officer said that when they did a background check on Jeff, he also had two outstanding warrants in Darby. One warrant was for assault and battery on a police officer and the other was for armed robbery. So, his bail was denied at the hearing they had that morning. I couldn't believe my ears. I just stood there with tears running down my face. I was embarrassed and ashamed that I had ever gotten involved with Jeff. Aunt Dee Dee said, "Don't cry. I knew that Joker was no good from day one, but I had to let you find that out for yourself. You acted like everything was fine whenever I came over there but I could tell you weren't happy. Why don't you and the baby stay with me, until you can get a job and get on your feet? I'll keep her for you while you work."

    I often wondered why Jeff insisted on going to the bus station in the middle of the night. He didn't want to run into the police as he knew he had warrants. This information was news to me. He never told me about his sordid past and I was so blindly in love, that I never paid attention to obvious signs that were big as life. I thanked God at that moment that Jeff and I were not able to get married when we went to City Hall with his grandmother that time with that hair brained scheme. I now see it as divine intervention. I am grateful that God doesn't always give us what we think we want.

I gave up the apartment and accepted my aunt's offer to stay with her. Our Christmas was sparse that year, but I was relieved and at peace. I was able to get a job right away and although I tried to give Aunt Dee Dee some money to help out she wouldn't take a penny. She was a great blessing to me.

Several months later, I decided I should make a trip to Philly and visit Jeff in jail to tell him that we were finished. (He had sent many letters to the apartment address that were forwarded to me by the post office). I wanted closure of that relationship. I didn't feel I could move on without facing him and letting him know that I had no intention of continuing our so called relationship.

As I sat across from Jeff with a Plexiglas separating us, he looked haggard and seemed to be a bundle of nerves. We both picked up the phone and Jeff started talking. "Hi honey, I'm so glad to see you, you look so good baby. Why haven't you written to me? I've been writing you almost every day. I miss you baby." Jeff's words of love no longer stirred me as they once did.

"Hello Jeff, I wanted to come in person to tell you that this is the only time that you will see or hear from me. I made a mistake Jeff; you are not the one for me. Dorian and I have moved from the apartment. Please don't write me anymore letters." "What are you talking about baby, you know I love you." "No Jeff, that's not love. When you love someone, you don't deliberately hurt them. I don't feel the same way about you anymore, and I wanted to tell you face to face. I wanted you to hear it from me first hand. It's over between us, and I'm not coming to see you again. I just thought I needed to tell you in person so there is no misunderstanding. We both need to move on with our lives."

Jeff cried and begged me to take Dorian and go stay with his grandmother in Darby. He was a nervous wreck. I felt sorry for him sitting there thin and haggard, begging and crying. Jeff's time was up and the guard came to search him and lead him back to his cell. He kept looking back as he was being led away, "Baby, please don't leave me."

I got up from the chair turned and walked quickly toward the door. I didn't want Jeff to see or misinterpret my tears. You see, I was crying too but not for the same reason. As I walked out into the cold fresh air, I took a deep breath. I was finally free. An overwhelming sense of relief and gratitude flooded my spirit. I was now able to look ahead toward my future with hope and great expectation. I looked upward and thanked God for answering my prayers and making a way for me, yet again.

//The End//

Author's Bio

Phyllis Clemmons holds a Bachelor's degree in Business Administration from Faulkner Christian University and a Master's Degree from Webster University in Management, Human Resource Development and Leadership. She has 45 years of combined public service in private, city and government sectors.

Phyllis had the privilege to teach Sunday school overseas as well as the United States. She is passionate in ministering a Godly word of encouragement to those who are sick, discouraged, down trodden and broken hearted. She has ministered in praise dancing as well as program designer for the Sisters In the Spirit Annual Retreat.

www.ingramcontent.com/pod-product-compliance
Lightning Source LLC
Chambersburg PA
CBHW051434290426
44109CB00016B/1545